JAMES E. MAGNER, JR.

136

JOHN
CROWE
RANSOM

MOUTON

DE PROPRIETATIBUS LITTERARUM

edenda curat
C. H. VAN SCHOONEVELD
Indiana University

Series Practica, 22

JOHN CROWE RANSOM

Critical Principles and Preoccupations

by

JAMES E. MAGNER, JR.

John Carroll University

1971

MOUTON

THE HAGUE · PARIS

LIBRARY OF CONGRESS CATALOG CARD NUMBER: 70.134542

Printed in Hungary

For
Charles R. Crow Jr.
Professor of English, University of Pittsburgh
and
John Crowe Ransom
Professor Emeritus, Kenyon College

ACKNOWLEDGMENTS

I thank Mary Ann Magner for her patience and help and Charles Crow for his sensitive and genial counsel during the writing of this work. I thank Miss Charis Newton, Mr. Elizabeth Catalano, Mr. Barbara Tackett and Mrs. Joan Lidrbzuch for the typing and the technical preparation of the manuscript. Finally, to the people of Mouton, I give my thanks for their interest and enthusiasm in the publishing of the work.

I give grateful acknowledgment to the following people and publishing companies for allowing me to quote excerpts from the copyrighted material listed below.

John Crowe Ransom, *The World's Body*. © 1938 by Charles Scribner's Sons; reprinted by permission of Charles Scribner's Sons, New York. John Crowe Ransom, *The New Criticism*. © 1941 by New Directions; reprinted by permission of New Directions Publishing Corporation, New York. John Crowe Ransom, *Poems and Essays*. © 1955, 1962 by Alfred A. Knopf, Inc.; reprinted by permission of Alfred A. Knopf, Inc., New York. John Crowe Ransom, essays from *The Kenyon Review*. © by Kenyon College; reprinted by permission of Kenyon College and John Crowe Ransom.

CONTENTS

I

INTRODUCTION

John Crowe Ransom is the critical champion of the existent in the world and in literature. This, it would seem, would be sufficient reason for the study of him. For if we do not know and revere existence, what do we know or revere? [Ransom believes that the world and the poem, which aesthetically reveals the world, should stand inviolate against the critical pragmatists of this age who "go about seeking whom they may devour" so that all things may become their image and their likeness. In short, Ransom is an objective rather than a narcissistic critic. He wishes the world and the poem to be perceived as what they are and not as someone would have them to be. He is in reaction against the critical tailors of the age who would cut the world and the poem to their own mental size, instead of letting the world, through the poem, increase the dimensions of their sartorial knowledge. Ransom is a critic who wishes to be faithful to the reality of 'the world's body', who wishes the poem aesthetically to reveal that reality, and wishes criticism to show the poem as revealing or distorting it. Those whom he calls the moral and scientific pragmatists seek to abstract from the world (that includes the poem) what is useful for their purpose and then order the world to their abstractions. For Ransom these are manipulators, not critics—interested in use, not revelation.

Ransom to a great extent fathered a 'new criticism' which was bent on letting the poem be itself and not something else; not, for example, a means of moral propaganda or psychic therapy. As critics, he and his followers are bent on letting the text reveal itself through the midwifery of the total concentrated powers of the reader. Ransom believes that in knowing this aesthetic being, the poem, we will more surely and deeply know its correlative—the world, in the fullness and realness of its 'body'.

let

This word 'body' is used deliberately by Ransom to connote the exquisite material being which constantly presents itself to the consciousness of man. Ransom is not a transcendentalist, an essentialist, or a mystic. He is a critic and a poet who is concerned with existent, particular being and man's revelation of it through the poem.

The new criticism, within whose ranks Ransom would include such critics as Cleanth Brooks, R. P. Blackmur, William Empson, Allen Tate, and to a qualified extent such critics as T. S. Eliot, I. A. Richards, and Yvor Winters, has brought the study of literature back to the classroom. The literature of history, instead of the history of literature, is now the topic for many teachers of English literature because of the written and classroom efforts of those critics.

In the following pages I hope to show the philosophical roots of Ransom's critical principles, to show these principles as they come to grips with the poem itself and to show Ransom's critical estimate of some poets and critics of his own time. Finally, I will try to show the reader where the critical strength and weakness of Ransom lie, where he seems to have erred and where triumphed.

Special emphasis will be given to Ransom's idea of the tensions and the structure of the poem itself. For example, I intend to treat his views of the poem as a tension of 'a prose core' and 'tissue of irrelevancy', as 'logical structure' and 'texture', as 'direct' and 'indirect meaning', as 'prose argument' and 'unstructured detail', and, finally, as 'metaphor, logic and meter'.

Ransom is worth the effort of this literary labor because he has persistently and enduringly given the poem back to the reader as a verbal being worthy of the reader's study. He also has left to the reader his critical tools, sharpened by years of dedicated scrutiny of poetic texts. He bestows his spirit upon us, a spirit of reverence for beings in the world, whether inside the poem or out, beings that he hopes will be understood and not warped by the energies of man.

II

JOHN CROWE RANSOM:
ONTOLOGICAL PARTICULARIST

A. RANSOM'S PLACE
IN THE ORIENTATIONS OF CRITICISM

In the first chapter of *The Mirror and the Lamp*, M. H. Abrams speaks of four general orientations that criticism has taken from the time of Aristotle to the present. The foundation for this division into four general orientations lies in the possible relationships of the work of literary art to the universe, to the artist, to the audience, and in the relationship of the matter to the form within the work itself. If the critic were preoccupied with the work of literary art as representing reality other than the artist's self, he would be a MIMETIC critic. If he were preoccupied with the work as affecting the audience pleasurably or morally, he would be a PRAGMATIC critic. If he were preoccupied with the work as configuring the interiority of the writer or as being caused by creative powers of the writer, he would be an EXPRESSIVE critic. And if he were preoccupied with the relationship of matter or content to form or execution, he would be an OBJECTIVE critic.

Speaking specifically, Aristotle by his identification of the poet with the imitator in the first chapter of the *Poetics*, Edward Young in his distinction between authentic and unauthentic imitation of style[1] and Lessing in his specifying that the special power of poetry lies in the reproduction of progressive action,[2] all would be MIMETIC critics.[3]

---

[1] Edward Young, *Conjectures on Original Composition*, ed. Edith J. Morley (New York, 1918).

[2] Gotthold Ephraim Lessing, *Laocoon*, trans. and ed. Edward Allan McCormick (New York, 1962), pp. 78–84.

[3] But Aristotle cannot be pigeon-holed, any more than other critics can be pigeon-holed. We talk here of critics' emphases and preoccupations.

Horace in his speaking of 'delectare', 'prodesse' and 'movere' as the ends or final causes of poetry, Sidney by his concern with the nurturing of virtue in man, and Johnson with his insistence on man's instruction by pleasure through imitation would fall predominantly into the PRAGMATIC orientation. Wordsworth[4] and Mill[5] by their definition of poetry, and Coleridge in his relation of poetry to the internal powers of the artist, such as the primary and secondary imagination, would be EXPRESSIVE critics. The twentieth century, however, has a strong claim on the bulk of the OBJECTIVE critics. For example, there is T. S. Eliot's insistence that when we are considering poetry, we must consider it primarily as poetry and not as something else and that the end of criticism is the elucidation of the work of art and not the poet's biography.[6] There is Cleanth Brooks' concern with the metaphor as the poetic embodiment of both matter and form.[7] There is also W. K. Wimsatt's and Monroe C. Beardsley's attack on both the 'intentional fallacy' and the 'affective fallacy' in *The Verbal Icon*.[8] And finally, there is John Crowe Ransom's[9] sharp anti-pragmatism in his assertions that the object of criticism is the poem as an autonomous work existing for its own sake.

By his interest in the structural properties of the poem, Ransom has aligned himself and other critics with a type of objective criticism, which he has termed 'The New Criticism'. Although Ransom says that Joel Spingarn, in introducing Benedetto Croce to the English public early in the century, was the first to use the term

---

In the *Poetics*, Aristotle is MIMETIC in his definition of poetry, PRAGMATIC in speaking of katharsis as the proper effect of tragic poetry and OBJECTIVE in considering the nature, the parts and the structure of the drama in itself.

[4] As the spontaneous overflow of powerful feelings in the *Preface to the Second Edition of the Lyrical Ballads*, eds. R. L. Brett and A. R. Jones (New York, 1963), pp. 235–266.

[5] As the feeling confessing itself to itself in his essay, "Thoughts on Poetry and Its Varieties", *Dissertations and Discussions* (London, 1905), I, 57.

[6] T. S. Eliot, "The Function of Criticism", *Selected Essays* (New York, 1950), p. 13.

[7] This theory is woven through the essays in *The Well-Wrought Urn* (New York, 1947).

[8] Chapters I and II are, respectively, devoted to these fallacies (New York, 1955).

[9] "Why Critics Don't Go Mad", *Poems and Essays* (New York, 1955), p. 150.

'new critic', Ransom is the man who gave the term its special current meanings by his work *The New Criticism*.[10] And he defines what he considers the fundamental consideration of the 'new critic' when he gives a qualified compliment to Yvor Winters, the perennial jouster with Ransom.

> Mr Yvor Winters is a victim of the moralistic illusion, but independently of that comes closer than anybody else I know to realizing what I should regard as the most fundamental pattern of criticism: criticism of the structural properties of poetry. The sciences deal almost entirely with structures, which are scientific structures; but poetic structures differ radically from these, and it is that difference which defines them.[11]

The new critic is the objective critic. He will regard the poem as an object that has in itself its own reason for being, because it artfully embodies the relation between subject matter and verbalized form. Thus, the critic should not be primarily concerned with the artist's intention or with the audience's response, but with the intelligible excellence of verbal execution. "A poem should not mean, but be."[12]

A further refinement of Abrams' objective orientation in criticism concerns what I call the ontological critic. This critic is rare, because large and deep minds are rare. And some minds are partly in and partly out of this category that requires a critic to have ultimate or philosophic reasons for his literary convictions and practices and to proceed critically under the influence of these reasons. Coleridge would be this type critic because his mind was animated by the metaphysics that direct his pronouncements. In the *Biographia Literaria*, he says, "I should call that investigation fair and philosophical, in which the critic announces and endeavors to establish the principles which he holds for the foundation of poetry in general."[13] In our own times, Jacques Maritain, Monroe C. Beardsley, and Eliseo Vivas would be ontological critics with a theoretical emphasis, and Northrop Frye, W. K. Wimsatt, and René Welleck would be ontological critics with a practical emphasis. They are all objective critics but with metaphysical width and depth of vision.

[10] John Crowe Ransom, *The New Criticism* (Norfolk, 1941), p. vii.

[11] *Ibid.*, p. xi.

[12] Archibald MacLeish, "Ars Poetica", *Collected Poems, 1917–1962* (Boston, 1962), p. 50.

[13] Samuel Taylor Coleridge, *Biographia Literaria*, ed. J. Shawcross (Oxford, 1907), I, 64.

Samuel Johnson would be an example of a critic who was NOT an ontological critic; T. S. Eliot and John Crowe Ransom would be examples of critics who only partly fulfill the requirements of the ontological critic. Though I have real and deep respect for Samuel Johnson as a man and a critic, I choose him as an example of a non-ontological critic for specific reasons and I give a metaphor to embody these reasons: Johnson was a taxi driver whose driving ability in a traffic jam was unparalleled, but who did not always know where he was going and where he came from. He did not really and clearly know the design of the city. Thus he would at times come to dead ends, but swerve dexterously and escape the critical fate of other less able drivers. On the other hand, Ransom and Eliot have learned the design of the city but do not always rightly and dexterously use the knowledge they have learned or seem to have learned so well.[14]

The ontological critic considers such questions as the nature of language, of art and beauty, and of the nature of poetry and the poem. He reasons about the end and the effect of art, the cause of art and inspiration, and knows the ultimate reasons why his answers are such and not otherwise. Eliot, however, does not always know these reasons[15] and neither does Ransom, as I shall illustrate in this work.

Thus, Ransom is what Abrams calls an objective critic, and what Ransom terms a new critic. He also participates in the method of the ontological critic, though not fully. His critical reasons are

---

[14] Both Ransom and Eliot were steeped in philosophy as students, Ransom at Vanderbilt and Oxford, Eliot at Harvard. In fact, Eliot did his doctoral dissertation on the philosophy of F. H. Bradley and had Josiah Royce as his advisor.

[15] For me, it is impossible to satisfactorily reconcile Eliot's impersonal theory of poetry, in "Tradition and the Individual Talent", (1919), which disclaims the substantial unity of the soul and his notion of ASSOCIATION (unity) or DISSOCIATION (disunity) of SENSIBILITY in "The Metaphysical Poets" (1927). The unified embodiment of emotive and cognitive experience in a poem would be a sign of excellence for Eliot, but if there is no unity in the efficient cause of poem (soul) how can there be unity in the effect (poem)? Furthermore, how can the poem be a proper objective correlative for the human person, having human emotions, if the human person does not exist as the creative cause of the poem? ("Hamlet and His Problems" — 1919). Either Eliot's theories or the principle of cause and effect must be in error.

not always driven to the foundations of thought, but one cannot deny that he has metaphysical dimension and that his critical insights have been born of philosophical meditation.

B. MAJOR METAPHYSICAL INFLUENCES ON RANSOM

John Crowe Ransom's metaphysical foundation is spread the distance of history: he is so eclectic in his conviction that I do not think that a biographer or critic will find a pure vein of any philosopher in him. What may seem a Kantian mind in one context will be empirical in the next. For example Ransom is Kantian in believing that art and the beautiful have '*Zweckmässigkeit ohne Zweck*',[16] but is not Kantian in his epistemological embracement of 'precious objects',[17] — believing that they surely are what they seem to be. Epistemology in this context is not problematic for Ransom.[18] Furthermore, Ransom is not 'willfully' idealistic, either subjectively (Kantian) or objectively (Platonic). The universal is very nearly a *flatus vocis* for him. Thus, Yvor Winters with some justice may term him a nominalist. Indeed, Ransom detests classification of the 'infinite' particular and, in this, also reminds one of the existential movement of the present day.

But in this survey of ultimate or philosophical influence, let us start at the beginning and look towards the present: Ransom is Platonic, but in an ironic way. That is, he has been affected by Plato but he reacts against this early affection; for example, his notions of existence, art and poetry rebel against Platonic idealism. If we understand Ransom in his anti-Platonism, we will have understood a great deal of the essential Ransom.

Ransom's fundamental insight — his very spirit as critic and his interest as human being — revolves about his dedication to the particular for the sake of itself. The ontological for Ransom is 'thing'; being is thing. Being is not thingness. Thingness is something that is necessary for knowing the 'precious or beloved object' but has

---

[16] Immanuel Kant, *Gesamelte Schriften, Der Critik der Urtheilstraft* (Berlin, 1910), Bd. V, erster Theil, erstes Abschnitt, erstes Buch, drittes Moment, No. 10, 220. I have used Kant's designations for this footnote.

[17] "Poetry: II, The Final Cause", *Kenyon Review* X (Autumn, 1947), 643.

[18] "The Concrete Universal: Observations on the Understanding on Poetry", *Poems and Essays* (New York, 1955), p. 182.

no value for Ransom in itself. The cognitive universal, the 'ens rationis' is not authentic being for Ransom; it is merely the outline of the 'world's body'. The 'world's body' in its fullness, in its exquisiteness, in its unpredictability and in its 'infinity'[19] is the real and proper object of the human mind, and only in union with the precious particular does the artist have the authentic aesthetic moment:

> Where is innocence then? The aesthetic moment appears as a curious moment of suspension; between the Platonism in us, which is militant, always sciencing and devouring, and a starved inhibited aspiration towards innocence which, if it could only be free, would like to respect and know the object as it might of its own accord reveal itself.[20]

The artist who looks with Plato's Demiurgos to the archetypes for the models of authentic existence configures illusion. It is in the stubborn and contingent objects of this world that the artist finds the matter for his poem. In this regard, Ransom says,

> Now the fine Platonic world of ideas fails to coincide with the original world of perception, which is the world populated by the stubborn and contingent objects, and to which as artists we fly in shame. The sensibility manifested by artists makes fools of scientists, if the latter are inclined to take their special and quite useful form of truth as the whole and comprehensive article.[21]
>
> . . . .
>
> The way to obtain the true *Dinglichkeit* of a formal dinner or a landscape or a beloved person is to approach the object as such, and in humility; then it unfolds a nature which we are unprepared for if we have put our trust in the simple idea which attempted to represent it.[22]

It may seem that too often Ransom identifies the abstraction of the scientist and of Aristotle with the ideas of Plato. Surely Plato would not like this nor would Sidney, Plotinus, and others who have had reverence for the 'foreconceit',[23] the exemplar cause as existing in the mind of man or the mind of God. The archetypes

----

[19] "Criticism, Inc.", *The World's Body* (New York, 1938), p. 348.

[20] "Poetry: A Note on Ontology", *The World's Body*, p. 130.

[21] *Ibid.*, p. 123.

[22] *Ibid.*, p. 124.

[23] We might distinguish here between the ULTIMATE foreconceit of GOD and the PROXIMATE foreconceit of MAN, both exemplar causes of different types of creation.

of Plato are not the abstractions of Aristotle. Aristotle is the father of abstractionism but Plato of recollection. For Aristotle, the universal was a cognitive synthesis abstracted from observed particulars; for Plato it was a primal form that gave particular things their qualities and their existence and that man could intuitively remember from a prior, spiritual existence.

Perhaps Ransom sometimes identifies the universal of Plato and the abstraction of Aristotle and the scientists because they reside, finally, in the mind as human conceptions which should never be an end in themselves. Yet, at other times, he will make sure and clear distinctions between Plato's deductivism and Aristotle's inductivism, indicating thereby his notion of the illusory and authentic sources of philosophy and of ideas in the mind of man. Considering criticism in relation to the Aristotelian and Platonic world view, he says:

> I must stop at this point, since I am desired not so much to anticipate the critic as to present him. In conclusion I will remark that the critic will doubtless work empirically, and set up his philosophy only as the drift of his findings will compel him. But ultimately he will be compelled. He will have to subscribe to an ontology. If he is a sound critic his ontology will be that of his poets; and what is that? I suggest that the poetic world-view is Aristotelian and "realistic" rather than Platonic and "idealistic." He cannot follow the poets and still conceive himself as inhabiting the rational or "tidy" universe that is supposed by the scientists.[24]

In this passage there is a truth that is partly submerged but that seems a *sine qua non* of authentic literary evaluation, namely, that the stylistic characteristics and the thematic concerns of a poet can best be arrived at by an inductive, not a deductive, process. That is, we must start with the texts and work up to a conclusion, rather than start with a conclusion and work down to the texts. AFTER we have induced the accurate universal from the texts, then we may proceed to new truths; but our universal concerning the characteristics or the themes in a poem or a poet will be true only if it is derived from the text. Our mind must focus upon the web of verbalization, thinks Ransom, not upon the recollection of ideas nor any other *a priori* concern. Allen Tate, his student at Vanderbilt in 1920, says of him, " . . . John Ransom was conducting

---

[24] "Criticism as Pure Speculation", *The Intent of the Critic*, ed. Donald Stauffer (Princeton, 1941), p. 124.

a revolution of his own in the teaching of literature. He was not an historical scholar and he was concerned, in talking about a literary work, with ideas and techniques. I was too ignorant to understand how it came about that such a man should be in an English department."[25]

There is in criticism no substitute for study of the text. Without it we derive imprecise universals and practice inaccurate criticism which a close-reading student will soon detect. The alternate method is what Northrop Frye calls 'narcissistic criticism', in which the critic finds what he wishes: himself and his own ideas.

Let me try to illustrate Ransom's method of teaching. Suppose a teacher were to say in class that one of Poe's defects of style was bathos in some of his poems. "Poe is sometimes bathetic" is his universal. Now, where is the foundation for the universal? If he has been an honest critic of Poe's poems he will have a sure foundation, because the universal's existence will have been derived from the textual particulars. "Lenore", whose jingle-jangle, jig-like rhythm does not sound like a dirge of one who mourns his beloved, might be offered as an excellent example of Poe's bathos: the unintended yoking together of the sublime and the ridiculous. Poe's apostrophic and dissonant use of anachronisms such as "Avaunt! Avaunt!", "Wretches!", "Peccavimus"; the bland combination of artificial tone and prominent internal rhyme—"Guy De Vere, hast thou no tear?"—simplifies itself into a notion of bathos. One stanza, here, will suffice:

> Wretches! ye loved her for her wealth,
>   and ye hated her for her pride;
> And, when she fell in feeble health,
>   ye blessed her—that she died;—
> How *shall* the ritual, then, be read—
>   the requiem how be sung
> By you—by yours, the evil eye,—by yours,
>   the slanderous tongue
> That did to death the innocence that died,
>   and died so young?[26]

I think Ransom would agree that the teacher's universal, here, has its ground in a text. Of course, there would have to be other

---

[25] Allen Tate, "For John Ransom at Seventy-Five", *Shenandoah*, XIV (Spring, 1963), 6.

[26] Edgar Allan Poe, "Lenore", *The Complete Works of Edgar Allan Poe*, ed. J. A. Harrison (New York, 1965), VII, 53.

examples, but this text would probably be a good beginning. And I think he would attack Poe not only on the basis of his loose rhapsodies but also on the basis of his Platonic subject matter. For Ransom's ontology, as noted above, is not of supernal otherness but of concrete thisness. And the sound critic for him must be anchored to thing, not to thingness, more to the HAECEITY of Duns Scotus than to the QUIDDITY of St. Thomas Aquinas—and never to the supernal forms of Plato or the supernal beauty of Poe. He believes that the world's body exists, and he derives his knowledge from sensate human contact with it.

Ransom insists that the sound critic's ontology be that of the poet, because he does not think that the world is tidy or systematized, but unpredictable and mysterious. And poetic experience is of this mystery and not of system. Secondly, he seems to imply that the precise critic must try to know the experience of the poet and how well the poet has expressed that experience, rather than try to endow the poet with his own ideas and experience. In short, the critic should think concretely in terms of reality, experience, and the text. Particularity is the source of critical verification.

Ransom says, "I suggest that the poetic world-view is Aristotelian and 'realistic' rather than Platonic and 'idealistic'. He [the critic] cannot follow the poets and still conceive himself as inhabiting the rational or tidy universe that is supposed by the scientists."[27] Here Ransom opposes Aristotle and his method to that of the scientists and Platonists, because Aristotle or the Aristotelians try to make faithful inductions from particulars, while the scientist and Platonist are more interested in making the world 'tidy' by schema or superimposed form. Although Ransom is not fond of generalizations, he may accept them if they have a foundation in concrete reality and are not created merely to rearrange the world. He thinks of this Platonic concern over the shape of things as idealistic pragmatism.

For Ransom, this notion of pragmatism is also embodied in the word 'tidy', because that is the condition in which Platonists suppose they can understand the world and precisely impose their dicta upon those who live in it, and it is also the condition in which the scientists can manipulate the world and saturate it with their practical concerns. When the world becomes 'untidy' it becomes

---

[27] "Criticism as Pure Speculation", *The Intent of the Critic*, p. 124.

universally unknowable and pragmatically unmanageable. But
Ransom is not interested in things being manipulated or managed.
Insofar as management will take care of basic human needs, it is
justified, but if the management becomes an end in itself and
'tidiness' is accepted as the optimum condition of human existence,
then man has arrived at a state which is inferior to the most
primitive. For in the primitive state man would at least know
things as they are and perhaps consider some things as too precious
to manipulate. Ransom is a dynamic conservative and a 'Fugitive' — he flees from the world in its technical obfuscation of reality
and in his mind and in his aesthetics contemplates the maze of
sensual objects through the 'manifold of sensation'.[28] He likes his
world complicated — he likes his 'twisted apples', for those are the
sweetest, though cast away by the market-minded farmer who
thinks of his prices and his gain.

Ransom will, at times, tolerate the Aristotelian because he
derives his principles from observation, he will even tolerate the
scientist if he supplies man with the necessary tools to live, but
he never tolerates the Platonist because there is no correspondence
between the notions in his head and the things in the world, and
because the Platonist viciously intends to reform the world in his
own image and likeness.

> Persons who are idealists by conviction, or on general principles, are
> simply monsters. (I mean the Platonic ones, the kind of idealists who worship
> universals, laws, Platonic ideas, reason, the 'immaterial.') Unlike the scien-
> tists, they are of no use, yet they willfully take upon themselves the dis-
> ability of the scientists, and not only do they have no pleasure in individual
> objects but they even solicit the public to make the same sacrifice. Pro-
> fessionally they tend to be philosophers, preachers, and educators, and from
> these positions infect us with their vice and keep us, in the range of our
> interest, more like animals and less like human beings than we have a right
> to be.[29]

. . . .

> They [idealists] would like to enforce an arbitrary simplification upon us,
> rather than to recognize a complication which exists. And that is repressive
> and antihumanistic, or, in short, it is vicious. We may assume that it is vain.[30]

---

[28] This 'manifold of sensation' will be ordered, in Kantian terms, by the
SENSIBILITY with its pure forms of SPACE and TIME (which are purely subjective). This total process is termed the 'Transcendental Aesthetic' by Kant
in his *Critique of Pure Reason*.

[29] "Sentimental Exercise", *The World's Body*, p. 225.

[30] *Ibid.*, p. 226.

In his essay "Address to Kenneth Burke",[31] Ransom traces the roots of this realistic criticism that likes its world and its texts uncomplicated. He makes his historical distinction between unauthentic and authentic philosophy and his derivative distinction between unauthentic and authentic critics. His basic distinction lies between the FIRST MOMENT OF PHILOSOPHY and the SECOND MOMENT OF PHILOSOPHY. The first moment of philosophy issued originally from the Eleatic philosophers such as Pythagoras, with his concern with mathematical order; it continued in Plato with his archetypes, flowed less strongly through Aristotle with his abstractions, reappeared in Kant with his transcendental ideas, intensified in Hegel and finally filtered into present-day criticism, in a work such as *The Philosophy of Literary Form* by Kenneth Burke. The second and more authentic moment of philosophy partly emerges in Kant, for he is, as it were, the bridge between the rationalists and the dynamically sensuous and nonpragmatic aestheticians, such as Schopenhauer, Nietzsche, Bergson, and Croce. These last have a sense of the 'world's body' as well as an idea of it. "It is with Philosophy II, not Philosophy I", says Ransom, "that we find all that is distinctive in poetry as compared with science, and in liberal education as other than the cult of science."[32]

Ransom thinks that Kenneth Burke's earlier criticism is lopsided for the same reason that Pythagoras' philosophy was lopsided: it is too logical and mathematical. Although Ransom has respect for Burke, "because his prose has literary distinction", and because "he has written wisely, and in advance of the rest of us, about the logic of figures, and some other purely poetic usages, to indicate participation in true aesthetics",[33] Ransom does not like Burke's emphasis on ideational content and its logical progression. The 'logical core' of the poem is not the whole poem—this would be coming dangerously close to what Brooks would call 'the heresy of paraphrase'.[34] Ransom puts it thus:

[31] *Kenyon Review*, XIV (Spring, 1942), 219–37.

[32] *Ibid.*, 224.

[33] *Ibid.*, 237.

[34] Cleanth Brooks, *The Well-Wrought Urn* (New York, 1947), Ch. XI. This argument also will be a partial foundation for Ransom's attack on Winters, in *The New Criticism*, where he describes Winters as 'The Logical Critic'.

To extend Kantian terms a little, I think the trouble with Burke's readings is his imagination plays too near the rational surface of the poem and the reason it does not go deeper is that he is no lover of nature. In the last resort, we shall not be talking intelligibly about art unless we can pronounce with warmth two terms that must have been odious to a proper Greek: love and nature. (I am talking 'poetically' now; Burke might say too 'poetically.')[35]

Furthermore, Ransom would not like Burke's notion that the authentic poem fulfills the psychic desire of the audience and he would not like Burke's 'one to one' relation between inner prior forms and the 'symbolic action' which is the poem. The first notion is too pragmatic, too therapeutic—it is Richardsonian;—the other is too formalistic.[36] The poet must disengage himself from the tidiness and security of formalism and any sort of dogmatism. He must have what Keats called 'negative capability'[37]—or what Nietzsche termed the hopefulness of free spirits. The poet must dwell in hopeful suspension and natural piety; he must be willing to believe that what he senses is true; he must rummage and stumble through the world's objects in courage and in love, believing that this is 'the best of all possible worlds', because it is the only one that exists or can exist for him. The poet must be willing to put up with the stubbornness and contingency of existence. He must not attempt to straight-jacket the world with procrustean universals in order to make it tidy and, thus, unreal.

I should say that we might call the poet's piety a "natural piety", his gift being for finding the natural world not merely mechanical but hospitable to the moral universalists . . . It is a horrid as well as a beautiful world, but without the horror, we should never focus on the beauty; without death there would be no relish for life; without danger, no courage, without savagery, no gentleness; and without the background of our frequent igno-

---

[35] *Kenyon Review*, XIV (Spring, 1942), 231. An interesting example of the Ransom dialectic is the contrast between this passage and the last four of five paragraphs in "More than Gesture", *Poems and Essays*, 107–8, where he takes R. P. Blackmur to task for concentrating too much on the 'how' and not enough on the 'what' of the poem, too much on the 'formal values' and not enough on the 'substantial values'.

[36] Yet, Ransom might well appreciate Burke's distinction between 'factual truth' and 'esthetic truth', in Burke's "Psychology and Form", *Counter Statement* (New York, 1931), pp. 38–56.

[37] John Keats, "Letter to George and Thomas Keats", *Keats' Complete Poetical Works and Letters*, ed. Horace E. Scudder (Cambridge, 1899), p. 277.

miny, no human dignity and pride. (These are excellent and rather Hegelian commonplaces.)[38]

Although one may be inclined to align himself with Ransom's statement, there is trouble in knowing just how the poet, for Ransom, will know and love the world. How shall the objects reveal themselves in their authenticity? It cannot be done through pure sense, because this excludes any spiritual or reflective cognition; it cannot be done through pure abstraction, for the universal is not the particular 'beloved' object; it cannot be done through 'recollection', for this is concern with the nonexistent archetypes.[39] What then is the power that will let the 'world's body' reveal itself to us? Ransom is not sure and explicit on this point. For some of us, as with Bergson and Croce and Maritain, the power that would enable man to encounter the existent being in existential experience would be cognitive intuition—that simple 'seeing' power which lies at the root of the soul's powers and yet incorporates at that root all of man's being.[40] Ransom is partly right when he speaks of the object of art as the particular or existent being, but he never really builds a needed bridge over his Cartesian abyss that exists between the mind and reality. He seems to be in a position similar to Kant's, and all he can say is that the synthesized action of the SENSIBILITY and the UNDERSTANDING[41] enables us to engage the existent objects, and that we must have faith that what we sense is true. The proof for this faith would be the world's 'sympathetic' response to our treatment of it. A kiss is a kiss, as long as there is the gift and the response. The touch of the beloved hand is really that touch, unless it feels like brambles. This is not a resolution of Ransom's epistemological problems;[42] yet it is a realization of which way Ransom tends to lead us.

[38] Ransom, "The Concrete Universal", *Poems and Essays* (New York, 1955), p. 183.

[39] I speak from Ransom's point of view.

[40] Jacques Maritain, *Creative Intuition in Art and Poetry* (New York, 1953), pp. 125–34. Benedetto Croce, "Aesthetics", *Encyclopedia Britannica*, 14th ed., rev. (Chicago, 1952), I, pp. 265–66. Henri Bergson, *The Creative Mind* (New York, 1946), pp. 107–29.

[41] For Kant, the manifold of sensations are ordered first by the SENSIBILITY with its pure forms of space and time, and secondly by the UNDERSTANDING with its twelve categories. The sensations are finally unified by REASON with its Transcendental Ideas of World, Soul and God.

[42] That is, objectively problematic to those who see a possible inconsistency in Ransom's theory of knowledge.

Let us move now to another problem that relates to Ransom's anti-Platonism: the problem of the nature of man and the nature of the experience embodied in the poem.

In his essay "The Inorganic Muses" Ransom gives his notion of what sort of human activity lies embodied in a poem:

> By this reasoning poetry is an organic-and-inorganic activity; first and last it is organic, or positive and in the service of the organism; in between, but discreetly and in less than subversive measure, it is inorganic, or un-related to the organic interest. It has a commanding identity with prose, and a radical but inimical difference.[43]

Ransom has gone to great lengths in this article to prove that there is something in man that is not merely organic. Organic in the context of this article means 'tangibly animal' and 'tangibly useful': a combination of these two. Ransom focuses, here, upon the muse that issues from loving concern with objects that have no concrete use. It is only with the utmost subtlety that Ransom can demonstrate, at least to his own satisfaction, that man is a little more than pure bulk and can have more than biotic, pragmatic motives. The man, even the dog, is able to have affection for his 'precious objects'. For man, these objects would be:

> For example, mother, mistress, child, the native landscape, the State, the ruler, the moon, the hearth-fire—I name the last as a sentiment already become "literary" and archaic in the degree that its utility has passed. We should be less than human if we did not confess to attachments for these objects quite disproportionate to their utility. We should be less than animal. A large part of the texture of a poem gets into it by simple citation of stock precious objects; the poet's understanding being that these objects already exist for us clothed in their imagery, and are ready-made for poetry.[44]

The reason Ransom has had great trouble and spent many words coming to this conclusion is that he is a naturalist, as he says, and has little confidence in finding the evidential activity of the soul of man. He has little patience with Platonic dualism—with Plato's metaphor of man as a soul imprisoned in a body or as an oyster imprisoned in its shell. The matter of poetry is a complex of precious objects which are appreciated, it seems, by animalistic affection, but not to serve animalistic ends. These objects are 'contemplated' for the sake of themselves. This animalistic contemplation is a con-fusion in Ransom, which I will let stay confused. He likens the dog's

---

[43] "The Inorganic Muses", *Kenyon Review*, V (Spring, 1943), 293.
[44] *Ibid.*, 292.

'inorganic' contemplation to the poet's contemplation when he says:

> The dog is like a poet in doing more than to expect and calculate his creature benefits from the objects; for example, the smell of the master's tobacco must be "vivid" to him yet without organic meaning. And the dog is a sort of religionist in the degree that the master's purposes and techniques remain inscrutable, and the dog's regard for them is speculative and humble.[45]

Platonic dualism has become passé for Ransom. Plato's teaching of the 'separable and immortal soul' and Aristotle's notion

> . . . of an intellect which works when the organism is not working, and independently of the organism . . . may have done noble service in defending our humanistic progress, but they have served their purposes . . . If it used to be that anthropologists were despicable cynics peeping and slandering in order to report animal origins behind the most exalted human activities, that was in my Platonic and metaphysical days. . . .[46]

Though he had called his work *God Without Thunder* (1930) an unorthodox defense of orthodoxy, this passage reveals him as not orthodox at all, in the Judeo-Christian sense. He is, here, a materialistic naturalist. His overwhelming interest is in the preciousness of particular being.

Despite all this affective naturalism and anti-soulism Ransom will laud John Donne as the archetype of the intellectual, no-nonsense masculine poet in contrast to Edna St. Vincent Millay,who lets her affections and meter get in the way of her 'logic'. He wants his poetry as T. E. Hulme wants it: hard, dry, mind-wrought, and restrained. He likes his masculine intellect embodied in the poem; he does not like the vague and pervading form of the feminine imagination. Ransom wants hard-wrought understatement, suggestions that in their subtle tension can later spring open or oscillate in the mind of the reader. He has little patience with vague affections and he chooses some famous and 'feminine' lines for righteous criticism:

> I burn my candle at both ends,
> It will not last the night,
> But ah, my foes, and oh, my friends,
> It gives a lovely light![47]

[45] *Ibid.*, 291–92.
[46] *Ibid.*, 284.
[47] "The Poet as Woman", *The World's Body*, p. 81.

Millay may have gotten away with these lines—especially the third—by her personally emotive and dramatic readings, but upon the dead page the poem does not have a chance against Ransom's incisive mind:

> But the gulf is too wide. The last two lines of the quatrain Donne could not have endured for their foolish ejaculations, so twinned yet laboriously varied, and for the poverty of the vulgar *lovely*. This is overwriting. To wish to make a thing look pretty or look smart is to think poorly of it in itself and to want it more conventional, and to try to improve it is to weaken and perhaps destroy it.[48]

The poem must have its 'logic', or it cannot have its 'tissue'; it must have its skeleton if it is to have its skin. Edna St. Vincent Millay does better in other poems, but in each case, Ransom 'shakes' the poems and down comes their structure. I think, in each case, he is justified. She does not give sufficient reason for the emotion she wants to evoke. She serves her emotion—as oftentimes does Shelley[49]—with little mind. In fact, Ransom, in a good example of his dialectic again, will take her to task for seeing too simply and too affectionately—with less than aesthetic distance— the 'precious objects' which are the object of the poem.

> For that matter, intellectual poverty has limited most poetry in all periods, whatever the gender of the authors, an evidence which would indicate that poetry has not really been the completely expressive art it is said to be. But the exceptional poetry which may properly be called express- ive, but which is popularly called intellectual, is not so rare but that we may know the real capacity of poetry as an instrument. It is a piano, a well- tempered clavier, and does not have to stick to the rules of the violin.
>
> It is not reduced to the picturization of simple and pleasant objects, though it is valuable when poets discover them, and especially at the back door, where Miss Millay found the pear tree blossoming

> "Like the waste-man's little daughter
> In her first communion dress."

Nor is it reduced to the display of the generous human passions, like the love of earth and God, as when she writes:

> "About the trees my arms I wound;
> Like one gone mad I hugged the ground;

[48] *Ibid.*, pp. 81–82.

[49] Elizabeth Atkins, whom Ransom is also criticizing, along with Edna St. Vincent Millay, asserts that a major influence on Millay was Hopkins, which I think is far from accurate. It is rather Shelley at his most sentimental and indefinite, not at his best.

I raised my quivering arms on high;
I laughed and laughed into the sky,
Till at my throat a strangling sob
Caught fiercely, and a great heart-throb
Sent instant tears into my eyes;
O God, I cried, no dark disguise
Can e'er hereafter hide from me
Thy radiant identity!"

These are earlier bits of poetry. It is with something of a feeling of guilt that the intellectual adult male participates in them. His heart wants to be in it but is not.[50]

Ransom thinks that Edna St. Vincent Millay has fallen victim to the tyranny of emotion and meter. And he may be right. He has induced sufficient reasons in this essay for attacking her poetry, and his choices of bad poetry have been judicious. Towards the latter part of the essay, he cites a few lines of the modern, masculine, intellectually gripped poetry that comes to earth with conscious reflective power. He contrasts this with Millay's poetry, which has little foundation in the 'world's body', and has not 'concretized' its 'universal'. He cites these lines to "quickly prove" that "there need not be an incompatibility between the man of intellect and the man of imagination"[51] and that the intellectual poet can be exquisitely lyrical.

The body dies; the body's beauty lives.
So evenings die, in their green going,
A wave, interminably flowing.
So gardens die, their meek breath scenting
The cowl of Winter, done repenting.
So maidens die, to the auroral
Celebration of a maiden's choral.[52]

And he cites lines by which the intellectual poet embodies an emotive attitude by a sharply sculpted 'concrete universal'.

I should have been a pair of ragged claws
Scuttling across the floors of silent seas.[53]

---

[50] *The World's Body*, pp. 98—99.

[51] *Ibid.*, p. 101.

[52] Wallace Stevens, second stanza of "Peter Quince at the Clavier", *ibid.*, p. 101.

[53] *Ibid.*, p. 102.

These lines are beyond Millay because she does not have that
strong grip on reality that is needed to make the poet great. In all
of this citing, Ransom does not spell out how one is to discern the
intellectual power that these lines supposedly hold; he supposes
this power to be evident to the reader.

[These] are not the most ambitious efforts of their authors, who are of
the living intellectualist poets; I have hit upon them hurriedly. But it is
my impression that Miss Millay has done no such passages as these. Intellectual power, with some of the skills that come from the intellectual dis-
ciplines, is written on them. The treasures too, for the field of reference is
too wide to be commanded by the innocent woman-mind, or for that matter
the man-mind which is not flexible enough to be at ease with its intellectual
attainments.[54]

He puts his attitude toward feminine poetry in a very succint
fashion on the fourth page of his essay, and if we understand
what he says here, we may well understand a great deal of the
new criticism in contrast to the affective criticism of the late and
middle nineteenth century. In this statement Ransom stands especially with Yvor Winters, whom he designates 'The logical critic'
in the *New Criticism*. The new critics are 'no-nonsense' critics:

For the devoted critic must maintain that poetry on whatever level
must make as consistent sense as prose, and he does not like being committed
in it to nonsense; it cannot be the idea of poetry to make us foolish, if that
is our habit, even though it must sometimes try to render something that is
elusive and hard to render.[55]

Though Ransom is impatient with Platonic dualism, he is, himself, a dualistic critic; his sight is Cartesian. After reading a Ransom
essay one thinks of a poem in terms of a nursery rhyme learned
long ago in school: "All the king's horses/And all the king's men/
Couldn't put Humpty together again." It is the 'prose core', the
'logical core', the 'structure' or the 'ego' in the poem versus the
'tissue of irrelevancy', the 'texture' or the 'id'. Indeed, in his dis-
avowal of Eliot's 'association of sensibility',[56] Ransom does not
view the poem as a unified correlative of the human personality.

[54] *Ibid.*

[55] *Ibid.*, p. 79.

[56] This would be a characteristic of poetic excellence for Eliot, in contrast
  tethe 'dissociation of sensibility' which was historically caused by the
omotive poet, Milton, and the cerebral poet, Dryden.

It is impossible for Ransom 'to feel his thought'. The poet thinks something and there accrues a 'tissue' of feelings or 'irrelevancy'.[57] The thought core and its emotive tissue are not unified psychologically for Ransom, and therefore cannot be unified poetically. The core of the poem may breed irrelevant associations, which if not too irrelevant will add to the fullness and intricate particularity of the poem. This tension — or really dualism in the poem — is correlative to the dualism in human experience where our feelings cannot at times be reconciled with the logic of our minds. In fact, Ransom cannot find the 'dissociation of sensibility' that Eliot said took place in the seventeenth century. Ransom sees this theory as a psychological absurdity and a historical inaccuracy.

I confess that I know very little about that; and I must add that, having worked to the best of my ability to find the thing Eliot refers to in the 17th Century poets, and failed, I incline to think there was nothing of the kind there. I have often tried — as what critic has not — to find some description of poetry which would regard it as a single unified experience, and exempt it from the dilemma of logic; but we must not like some philosophers become the fools of the shining but impractical ideal of "unity" or of "fusion." The aspiration here is for some sort of fusion of two experiences that ordinarily repel one another: the abstracted exercise of reason in hard fact and calculation; and the inclusive experience of literally everything at once. But we cannot have our theory magical and intellegible at the same time. For it would seem that from that precise moment when the race discovers that what has seemed to be an undifferentiated unity is really a complex of specialized functions, there can be no undifferentiated unity again; no return. We do not quite know how to feel a thought. The best we can do is to conduct a thought without denying all the innocent or irrelevant feelings in the process. The dualism remains.[58]

One might remark, here, in response to Ransom's criticism of Eliot's thesis that tension in the poem or in the poet implicity proves the existence of unity and that the testimony of consciousness bespeaks a unity that perdures through the complexity of experience. Has Ransom erred by emphasis, by making the distinction between thought and feeling a dichotomy? Indeed, Eliot may have realized an authentic limitation in Dryden since Dryden sarcificed the power of emotively suffused intuition for the hard logic of the

[57] "T. S. Eliot, the Historical Critic", *The New Criticism* (Norfolk, Conn., 1941), p. 184.

[58] *Ibid.*, p. 183–84.

discursive power. Though in the name of satire, he restrained warmth for the sake of cognitive progression. But Eliot has erred in thinking that Donne best accomplished 'the association of sensibility'. The skeleton of Donne's logical progression and highly cerebral comparisons sticks through the 'flesh' or the 'tissue' of his poetry. Donne is a poet who comes very close to fulfilling the dualism that Ransom insists exists in a poet and his product. There is both a hard 'core or logic' in Donne's poems and a very intense breeding of emotion. A Donne poem is like a warm-blooded yet lean man, who stands before you, making you aware of his passionate intensity and his sharp, angular structure.[59]

In the preceding paragraphs of this chapter, I have wished to give the reader a sense of the nuances and the paradoxes of Ransom's anti-Platonism. It is not really a 'pure' anti-Platonism, for what he rejects as folly, he sometimes participates in. Ransom's thought is evolving and dialectical; he is paradoxical and, at times, partly contradictory. But this is a characteristic which makes him a vital critic; he will not close himself off from new notions, he will not wean himself on principles which have lost their sustenence, though this disengagement may lead to darkness or even to error. I have tried to show his reaction against disembodied formalism, against pragmatic formalism and even against Platonic dualism, to which he himself is particularly prone.

It remains an interesting tension in Ransom that he minimizes the spiritual principle in man, "the separable immortal and inorganic soul", as being distinct from the body, but sees a dualism existing between emotion and intellect both in the poem and in the poet. One does not "feel his thought", says Ransom, and the 'structure' of the poem is not its 'texture'. Yet if the effects are supposedly of different kinds must not their cause also be of different kinds? If the nature of the emotion is different from the nature of the idea, must not the cause or principle of the emotion also be different from that of the idea? Using Ransom's dualistic premise of separate effects, one comes to a conclusion of separate

---

[59] Here I think Eliot falls prey to the critical claws of Ransom, for Donne is indeed a masculine, intellectual poet. (Yet not to the extent that his sensibility is 'dissociated' so that there is not a relatively unified being giving relative unity to a poem. Indeed, without a degree of harmonic unity, the work cannot be said to be a poem.)

causes. Perhaps Ransom thinks of emotion and ideas as being different acts in degree, not in kind; this would allow him an exit from this seeming inconsistency. Yet, his theory of dichotomies leaves him open to the attack of perceptive critics.

Let us pass now to a brief consideration of other thinkers who have influenced Ransom in other essential ways. In this consideration, we shall focus upon a central insight in each man that has influenced Ransom's total attitude toward existence or his specific attitude towards literature. We shall pass over Hegel and Kant because these philosphers will be taken in the second chapter, which will treat 'the concrete universal'.

C. OTHER METAPHYSICAL OR ULTIMATE INFLUENCES

In the fourth part of his essay "Art and Mr. Santayana", Ransom concerns himself with man's devouring appetite toward the objects of this world and with the answer of two philosophers to this 'unmannerly ferocity of man as animal'. The last sentence of the following passage is of real significance to one who wishes to know Ransom as a man responding to existence and as a critic responding to literature. This sentence and this theme thread their way throughout the essays of Ransom. It is an insight which modifies the focus of his mind.

If Mr. Santayana as a free personality in a dull professional world reminds us of Emerson, in the light of his systematic philosophy he is a diffused modern version of Schopenhauer. Both are very well aware of the customary unmannerly ferocity of man as an animal, with Schopenhauer of course grieving more than tolerant Mr. Santayana about that; the animal directing and corrupting the most remote-looking and publicly esteemed pursuits, like tribal morality, which passes for disinterested action, or science, which passes for the pursuit of pure knowledge; yet kennelled, or put to sleep, or transcended, in at least one free and charming activity, which is aesthetic experience. In art, according to Schopenhauer, we at last have knowledge without desire.[60]

Schopenhauer nurtured Ransom's conviction that the world is not to be devoured if we are to be happy. It is in art, Schopenhauer says, that we retreat to the eye of cool serenity within the disturbed and rushing vortex of the world. Here we contemplate

[60] "Art and Mr. Santayana", The World's Body, pp. 324–25.

the 'precious object' as 'will-less subjects of knowledge'.[61] Schopenhauer believes that only in the contemplation of art or in the
ascetic's contemplation of God's otherness can man transcend
himself and thus not suffer. It is in the losing of oneself in the
object of art for the sake of itself—for its objective beauty—that
we will be released from the gnawing of the ego and its desires.
Indeed, man goes from desire to desire and from the abatement
of one pain to the onset of another. He desires his dinner and has
his dinner and is bored and desires again not to be bored. But in
the transcendence of finite will in contemplation—and in the
ecstasis that results—he is lifted out of self and into a state similar
to the 'ataraxia' or 'nirvana' of the Stoics and the Buddhists.

The result of man's constant desire, for Ransom, is man's constant pragmatism: the manipulation of the objects of the world
for ends beyond themselves. This pragmatism is spurred not only
by animal appetites but also by the ethical will that wishes to put
things in order. In accordance with this theory, Ransom distinguishes between the ethical consideration of reality and the poetic
consideration of reality. The presence or absence of the ethical will
in verbal discourse is a distinguishing characteristic between prose
and poetry. In poetry, man seeks 'knowledge without desire';
in prose man seeks knowledge with an end beyond itself. Man
transcends his devouring will and his 'unmannerly ferocity' in
the contemplation of art:

> It is highly probable that the poem considers an ethical situation, and there
> is no reason why it should repel this from its consideration. But, if I may say
> so without being accused of verbal trifling, the poetic consideration of the
> ethical situation is not the same as the ethical consideration of it. The straight
> ethical consideration would be prose; it would be an act of interested science,
> or an act of practical will. The poetic consideration, according to Schopen-
> hauer, is the objectification of this act of will; that is, it is our contemplation
> and not our exercise of will, and therefore qualitatively a very different
> experience; knowledge without desire.[62]

Ransom believes that the thing written in the poem is infinitely
precious to the poet, and, if it is not, the thing written is really not
a poem, but some sort of end-beyond-itself schematization. The poet
for Ransom, rummages lovingly through the world's objects

[61] Arthur Schopenhauer, *The World as Will and Idea*, trans. R. B. Haldane
and J. Kemp (London, 1891), I, 270.
[62] "Criticism as Pure Speculation", *The Intent of the Critic*, pp. 99–124.

attempting to know the 'world's body' and its parts until some of it becomes 'familiar' enough to be loved and written about for its own sake.

By precious I mean: beyond price or valued at more than the market value of such objects. . . . A precious object is a familiar one, yet it is always capable of exhibiting fresh aspects of a substance which is contingent and unpredictable. . . . It is what certain philosophies now call an "existent"— though not an odious one, as some of them prefer to have it. It is a sizable object, and a comparatively permanent one; we leave it and come back to it; we may even call it, speaking comparatively, an absolute object, since it persists full-bodied and unchanged in the midst of what is confused and shifting. We cherish it precisely in its absoluteness and inviolability.[63]

Ransom does not side, however, with Schopenhauer's notion that the world is Idea made multiple and that the artist embodies the Platonic idea.[64] Schopenhauer's artist is Platonic; he moves creatively from the contemplation of the Idea of some aspect of existence and configures this Idea in the body of the artefact. Ransom's artist is Aristotelian (in the wide sense): he contemplates only the 'world's body' in its infinite particularity and tries to come to a knowledge which results in 'structure' and a feeling which results in 'tissues of irrelevancy'.

To speak of Benedetto Croce may be more pertinent than to speak of Arthur Schopenhauer in relation to Ransom. For Schopenhauer's concern with existence is not identical with his concern with art and beauty, though these hold an essential position in his idea of existence. But Croce is an aesthetician who is concerned with existence from the aspect of art and beauty. And he is intensively concerned with the creation of the poem as a species of art, and what the poem is when it is made.

We know that Ransom read Croce and that he gave Kant and Croce credit for initially modifying his views towards poetry in particular and art in general. This modification probably came after Ransom's undergraduate years of concentration in classics and Greek philosophy at Vanderbilt University (1903–06) and after his discussions with Christopher Morley, a fellow student at Oxford,

---

[63] John Crowe Ransom, "Poetry: II, The Final Cause", *Kenyon Review*, IX (Autumn, 1947), 643–44.

[64] WILL would be the full activization of objectivization of IDEA in world. It would be the Idea in full, dynamic act. Arthur Schopenhauer, *The World as Will and Idea*, I, 271–74; see also *The World's Body*, pp. 45, 325.

who introduced him to the concrete delights of modern poetry. Allen Tate makes interesting mention of Ransom's background in 1920, when Tate was Ransom's student at Vanderbilt.

> I doubt that he had taken more than two or three courses in English as an undergraduate at Vanderbilt; he took none at Oxford [though he became interested in it through discussion groups] where he read the Greats, ancient history and philosophy. He was an excellent classical scholar. . . .
>
> . . . .
>
> John Ransom's grounding in Greek philosophy led him on to read the modern philosophers, and he was, at that time, an evowed Kantian. We heard a good deal, indirectly, about *The Critique of Judgment* and *Nicomachean Ethics*.[65]

Ransom mentions his disenchantment with Aristotle's poetics and his early re-education by Kant and Croce in his essay "Humanism at Chicago".

> And there was a time when I, for example, like a good many young men I knew, could not endure to listen to disparagement of my philosopher. I knew the *Nichomachean Ethics*, and used it for years as a sort of Bible. But when I got seriously into the *Poetics*, my veneration was a little chilled. The work did not seem commensurate with my literary speculations; by that time I had at least read Kant and Croce. And now that my own age has witnessed a flood of importunate writings by spirited critics, I do not turn back and sound Aritsotle upon certain of our stock preoccupations with literature without making the depressing discovery that he is unfamiliar with them; and, presently, that if I try to force from him some pronouncement by implication, the starch starts going out of the whole business; clearly this is not the way to proceed in it. We still have to search out the mysteries as they offer themselves, and from where we stand.[66]

As early as 1929 there is textual evidence of agreement between Ransom and Croce. He lauds Croce for thinking that art has authentic value in itself, that its very particularity or uniqueness gives it its worth, and that it needs no canonization by the 'pedagogues' who wish to use it for their own peculiar ends.

> But whether it [art] is post-scientific, or prescientific, Signor Croce is surely right in regarding it as un-scientific, and in defending the absoluteness or particularity of its representations. This absoluteness at once repels the effort of the pedagogue, pulpiteer, or other idealist to identify the work of art with some 'meaning' dear to himself. The work of art is its own infinite self, containing that meaning, but not at all reducible to it, keeping its

---

[65] Allen Tate, "For John Ransom at Seventy-Five", p. 6.
[66] "Humanism at Chicago", *Poems and Essays*, pp. 92–3.

meanings like any other particular. It would seem that the artist as well as the metaphysician has a gift for looking upon reality.[67]

For Ransom as well as Croce, man must realize the concrete if he is to realize reality. Ransom would emphasize the infinite particularity, the exquisite fullness of the thing in itself as an end in itself. Croce—a dynamic idealist—would not be content to rest solely in the particular, but he would insist that man can only come to a realization through the evolved and spiritualized particulars of this world. Both would say that man's knowledge and man's creative act do not center about or spring from Platonic archetypes, disembodied abstractions or innate ideas. Man must return to— must intuit—the particular, in order to create the unique. In the following passage Croce distinguishes between the unauthentic and the authentic *a priori* notion. The unauthentic—or really non-existent—*a priori* notion is the Platonic archetype that exists in absolute independence from developing or evolving matter. The authentic *a priori* notion is derived from the realization or the creation of a particular object: Yeats, Croce might say, knew "The Lake Isle of Innisfree" as poem only in the moment of its verbal creation as poem. The idea of something is 'awakened by its marriage with matter. The idea is born incarnate. "Rem tene, verba sequentur; if there are no verba, there is no res."[68] And this idea is never static but always dynamic, for matter and existence are dynamic for Croce:

> But it is desirable to dispel the illusion that this concept [of art] exists as an innate idea, and to replace this by the truth, that it operates as an *a priori* concept. Now an *a priori* concept does not exist by itself, but only in individual products which it generates. Just as the *a priori* reality called Art, Poetry or Beauty does not exist in a transcendent region where it can be perceived and admired in itself but only in the innumerable works of poetry, of art and of beauty which it has formed and continues to form, so the logical *a priori* concept of art exists nowhere but in the particular judgments which it has formed and continues to form. . . .[69]

Yet art's creation, for Ransom, is not a primitive, pre-adult, simple experience as he thinks it is for Croce. Art, for Ransom, is a rebellion of man against technology—a longing for the existential

[67] John Crowe Ransom, "Flux and Blur in Contemporary Art", *Sewanee Review*, XXXVII (Sept., 1929), 363.

[68] Croce, "Aesthetics", *Encyclopedia Britannica*, pp. 256–66.

[69] *Ibid.*

root of things. The artist is a fugitive, fleeing the commercial, pragmatic, and rationalistic jungles of modern man. Man has matured after he has experienced science (the logical endeavor with an end beyond itself), has rejected it as a way of life and has gravitated to the love and artistic creation of things in themselves. Thus, art is 'post-scientific' and adult, not 'pre-scientific' and childlike.

Art has always been devoted to the representation of the particularity which real things possess, and therefore it has always been a witness against the claims and interests of science. Signor Croce is in error, it seems to me, in assuming that art is simple child's-play, with its visions and representations; for it seems certain that art, as a usual thing, is late, post-scientific, rebellious against science, and bent on exposing to scorn the little constants of our scientific thinking when it compares them with the infinites of quality with which they are invested in reality. Art is complex and not simple in its psychology, adult and not infantile; and back of art there is the embittered artist, whose vision of the real has been systematically impaired under the intimidations of scientific instruction, and who seeks with indignation as well as with joy to recover it.[70]

Whether art is 'post-' or 'pre-scientific', both Ransom and Croce believe that poetry, as a species of art, is not the turbid emotionalism for which Ransom criticized Edna St. Vincent Millay. Though the poem is 'lyrical intuition'[71] this intuition must be realized in the conversion of feeling into images within poetic form. "Art is not feeling in its immediacy"[72] but it is "feeling altogether converted into images".[73] It is the structure of the poem, not the feeling of the author, that must stand the test of evaluation. The object of criticism is an objective, formal, verbalized being that has its structure of logic, embodied in its tissue of images.

In the following passages, we also can see Croce's and Ransom's shared distaste for the affective immediacy of Romanticism, and their shared insistence on artistic form and aesthetic distance. By 'affective' Croce means, in the following passage, man's emotive, and not yet organized, response to existence.

The problem for aesthetics today is the reassertion and defence of the classical as against romanticism: the synthetic, formal theoretical element which is the *proprium* of art, as against the affective element which it is

---

[70] "Flux and Blur", 362.
[71] Croce, p. 264.
[72] *Ibid.*
[73] *Ibid.*

the business of art to resolve into itself, but which today has turned against it and threatens to displace it.[74]

. . . .

Given an object, and a poet burning to utter himself upon it, he must take into account a third item, the form into which he must cast the utterance. (If we like, we may call it the *body* which he must give to his passion.) It delays and hinders him. In the process of "composition" the burning passion is submitted to cool and scarcely relevant consideration. When it appears finally it may be said to have been treated with an application of sensibility. The thing expressed there is not the hundred percent passion at all.[75]

We have lastly, in Croce's aesthetics, more than a hint of Ransom's critical notions. For example, his theories of moral and concrete universal were suggested by Hegel and 'focussed' by Kant,[76] but Croce's notions of the poem as the embodiment of 'moral consciousness',[77] his demand for logic in the poem and his realization that logic is not poetic language, all have implicit likenesses to Ransom's conception of art and the making of the poem. Ransom's notion of the lyric as being the supreme type of poetry may also have some foundation in the writings of Croce.[78]

I have attempted, in a brief way, to show a few similarities between the aesthetics of Croce and the criticism of Ransom that point to the influence of Croce on Ransom. I have done this to elucidate a very possible cause-and-effect relation and to create a further theoretical dimension in which to place Ransom's critical theory. Sigmund Freud, whom I will presently treat, is a definite and demonstrable influence on the criticism of Ransom. And if we understand Freud's terms of psychology, we will more deeply understand this phase of Ransom's criticism.

In the summer of 1947, Ransom wrote an article for the *Kenyon Review* that indicates some modification of his critical ideas. In fact, the period from 1947 (when he wrote "Poetry I: The Formal Analysis") to 1955 (when he published the "Concrete Universal:

---

[74] *Ibid.*, p. 265. See also *The World's Body*, pp. 31 and 291.

[75] *The World's Body*, p. 40.

[76] See *Poems and Essays*, p. 163.

[77] Croce, p. 264. Croce means by 'moral consciousness' man's conscious involvement in mankind and existence: man as authentically and committedly human.

[78] Croce, p. 264. See also "Mr. Empson's Muddles", *Southern Review*, IV (Autumn, 1938), 337.

Observations on the Understanding of Poetry") seems to be more a transition period for Ransom than any other. These dates are not lines of demarcation but they are approximations of the dawn and dusk of an era of dynamic modification. It is in this period that Ransom begins to analyze the poem in terms of Freudian psychology, that he is more inclined to understand Winters' 'moral' poetry as being 'plausibly' human[79] and that he is more inclined to accept the universal in terms of 'moral consciousness'[80] and its embodiment as the 'concrete universal'. In short, he is moving somewhat away from the idea that poetic criticism must be wholly a formal, objective, linguistic analysis. It must be this; but it must be more. Is the poem 'the waking dream'[81] of Kenneth Burke? Perhaps a 'waking dream', but now in terms of the author, not the audience. It occurs to him "to regard the poem as a work on the order of a Freudian Dream, having not only a 'manifest' and permissible content but a "latent and suspected content".[82] The logic and the texture have now been transmuted into the 'ego' and the 'id' levels of poetry. The id level of the poetic language is embodied in the 'substantival excrescences' which ooze out despite the censory logic of the ego. The task of the poet now is to rationalize the id-motive to the extent that it becomes intelligible in language. The task of the critic is to understand this process as embodied in the poem. How does the ego organize the id and how does the id make more interesting or 'substantival' the verbal operation of the ego?[83]

Ransom says,

Let us see what we can do if at once we take the thought-work to be the ego's, the play upon substance to be the id's. Our task is then, if possible, to rationalize the id-motive; that is to see what there might be in the situation of the organism, unknown to immediate consciousness, which would justify the peculiar interest of the id if the id could speak for itself.[84]

---

[79] Yvor Winters, *In Defense of Reason* (Denver, 1947), p. 528.

[80] Croce, p. 265.

[81] Kenneth Burke, "Psychology and Form", *The Dial* (July, 1925), 34–46.

[82] John Crowe Ransom, "Poetry I: The Formal Analysis", *Kenyon Review*, IX (Summer, 1947), 441.

[83] John Crowe Ransom, "Poetry II: The Final Cause", *Kenyon Review*, IX (Autumn, 1947), 654.

[84] *Ibid.*

Ransom says "I am not a technical Freudian, not knowing the system closely though I have read some fundamental texts repeatedly. And I am not an orthodox Freudian, since I do not feel impelled to embrace the precise teachings of Freud, nor some 'official' set of doctrines approved by a set of Freudians."[85] But he goes on to say that Freud would have relished the psychic tension of Antony's funeral oration before the people of Rome, where the ego assents to Brutus' command but the id 'oozes' through in terms of tone, of innuendo, of ambiguity, and of timing. Indeed, the id of Antony as verbalized in his oration destroys Brutus and his hopes for a republic. Yet the blind desire and the fire of hate in Antony are contained by the ego to the extent that the oration can be called 'manifestly' or 'explicitly' or 'logically' a funeral oration and not a passionate exhortation to rebel.[86]

This is not a different Ransom, but I think it is a Ransom with a slightly altered disposition and a different set of tools. The object of criticism is still the text, but the text with more intentional and psychological reference.

D. THE SIGNIFICANCE OF RANSOM'S ONTOLOGICAL CRITICISM AND YVOR WINTERS' REACTION TO IT

This mention of Ransom's critical modification by Freudian psychology is a good point at which to enter into the last problem of this chapter: whether or not Ransom's 'particular ontology' is worthwhile. Yvor Winters thinks not, because Ransom ultimately stands for nothing stable: the very basis for Ransom's criticism (particular being) is in constant flux. Ransom cannot believe in stable universals. Thus, Winters believes him to be both a nominalist and a relativist. He is the mouthpiece of critical and ontological chaos. His criticism is 'Thunder Without God',[87] a whirlwind without a stable center.

To be more specific, Winters' argument is this: that if Ransom by-passes the universal, ignores its authentic, though general, representation of particular reality, and pays attention only to

---

[85] "Poetry I: The Formal Analysis", 448.

[86] *Ibid.*

[87] Yvor Winters, "John Crowe Ransom or Thunder Without God", *In Defense of Reason* (Denver, 1943), pp. 502–55.

multiplicity, not to universal unity induced from multiplicity, there can be no conversation, no argument, no thought about poetry, poems or any other reality. Man thinks only by predicating the universal of the particular. One man authentically communicates with another, thinks Winters, only if both men have the same idea or concept of a thing or class of things in their minds. If they are thinking of two different things, then dialogue is fruitless; they are really holding quasi-soliloquies. Winters does not think that men can know the individual thing in itself, but he would incline towards Aquinas' notion of moderate realism: that a universal really does exist in the mind, and that this universal has a foundation (but not a corresponding universal) in the reality of particulars. It seems to me, that Ransom OPERATIONALLY is a moderate realist, though he would like to know things in their 'precious particularity', and this leads him into epistemological difficulty. OPERATIONALLY, he is a moderate realist; DISPOSITIONALLY — and therefore, at times, textually — he is a nominalist, as Winters claims. Let me give excerpts of Winters' argument.

Ransom is a nominalist, at least in intention, and as far as may be by persuasion, although the entire business gives him a good deal of embarrassment. It would be only with hesitation and regret that he would admit that he and I both are men and that the concept *man* is of the first importance if we are to be understood; this in spite of the fact that he and I are able to conduct an argument on what we take to be the same subject, and, when all things are considered, to understand each other fairly well; in spite of the fact that neither one of us, I imagine, would offer occasion for much astonishment either to an anatomist or to a psychologist.[88]

. . . .

. . . One can say nothing about any object, be it unique or not, except in words, that is through the subdivision and interrelation of abstractions — not by the object but by our understanding of the object . . .[89]

The difficulty with Ransom's position is this: that he knows, finally, that he cannot get rid of abstractions, yet he has an abhorrence of the rational processes which is less related to that of Ockham than to that of the romantics; it is a traditional feeling — I refer to romantic tradition — which makes him abhor words such as *moral*, *ideal*, or *rational* without troubling really to understand what they mean. As a result, he tries always to theorize about poetry, as if he had actually got rid of the general as a vicious delusion, and sometimes he actually does so theorize. But he has not got rid of it, and it makes him a great deal of trouble.[90]

[88] *Ibid.*, p. 510.
[89] *Ibid.*, p. 512.
[90] *Ibid.*, p. 513.

I think that Winters has driven through a weak spot in the Ransom armor: Ransom's epistemology. And Winters' lance has been the strong weapon of his logic. On the discursive level of cognition, I see no way out of Ransom's dilemma: man simply knows by abstraction and the predication of abstraction on the particular, for instance, "A rose is beautiful" or "That horse is dead". But on another level, which is the authentic poetic level, Ransom does have an out — that of intuition. Cognitive intuition is not problematical, it is not discursive — it is that most simple seeing power of the human being that dwells at the root of the soul's power that knows immediately, not mediately, the existent thing.

By intuition, I mean the immediacy of existential perception. I do not mean the material progression from one point to another, which, in the logical realm, is termed discursive reasoning. I do not mean the jumping logically from one stone to another across the river of problematic extension; I mean vision if the object is immaterial; penetration, if the object is material. Yet the most authentic word for both types of intuition is perception.

By intuition we plumb the depths of Being — we become divers who touch the bed of the ocean of Being, and nothing can replace that touch; we have not figured out the depth of the ocean and what the texture of its bottom is by means of instruments; we know it. We do not talk ABOUT a subject, we penetrate into the subject. We are not outside our subject, describing it; we become, spiritually digest it and figure it forth in the magic of words, originating in intuition.[91] Here, on this level of immediate perception, Ransom escapes the hard lance of Winter's logic. In conceptual progression we must predicate, but in poetic experience, we may only and simply perceive. To fall in love and to write of it, is not the resolution of a problem or the unravelling of a syllogism. As for Ransom's relativism which flows organically from his dedication and preoccupation with the world and its 'precious objects', I do not think that he is particularly 'embarrassed' by it.

I think that we may have a good inadvertent description of both Winters and Ransom, as critics, in R. P. Blackmur's essay "A

[91] I have here repeated some thoughts in an article of mine "Towards a Definition of Poetry", XII, *Fine Arts* (May 30, 1965), 4–5.

Critic's Job of Work".[92] For Blackmur, criticism is "not a light but a process of elucidation" and "the worse evil of fanatic falsification is when a body of criticism is governed by an *idée fixe*, a really exaggerated heresy, when a notion of genuine but small scope is taken literally as of universal application".[93]Although Winters' notions are not 'small in scope', he himself can be called what Blackmur terms a 'literalist'. He believes in absolute values. But that absolute values exist and that we can know them as they exist are two different questions which are often confused. Some people who assert the existence of absolute truths, implicitly assume in that assertion their possession of an absolute intellect. This is obvious error and not so subtle pride. The man of 'absolute' knowledge never changes his mind. And the 'man' who never changes his mind is either an idiot or God (at least, unto himself). In both cases, he is in trouble. I do not want to oversimplify and say that Winters is static and Ransom dynamic, for Winters depends upon observation for his notion of 'plausible morality' and Ransom has always had his prejudice against science and idealistic philosophy. But it would seem that Ransom would have the disposition dynamically to improve his theories where Winters would not. Ransom has a disposition to openness that can bring critical potency into act; Winters' disposition may be to maintain what is already in act and not move further into a deeper realization of aesthetic existence. I do not think that Ransom is overanxious about people's knowing he changes his mind; Winters may be. I think Ransom commits himself to change when he commits himself to the particular, when he opens himself to existence as evolving. I think that Ransom has great doubts about the permanence of dogma and would identify dogma with myths of psychic need.[94] And for him, myth is a thing which has grown in the minds of men because there is a need in their being for its realization and its ritualization. In this sense, he cannot be called an orthodox Christian, certainly not a fundamentalist or any sort of literalist or absolutist. Ransom's strength and his weakness are in his tentativeness; Winters' strength and weakness are in absoluteness. One

[92] R. P. Blackmur, "A Critic's Job of Work", *The Double Agent, Essays in Craft and Elucidation* (New York, 1935), pp. 269–302.

[93] *Ibid.*, p. 278.

[94] See John Crowe Ransom, *God Without Thunder, An Unorthodox Defense of Orthodoxy* (New York, 1930), p. 81.

assumes that because he does not know surely, surety does not exist; the other assumes that because absolutes exist, he knows them as existing. Let us say at any rate that these men lean respectively in these two directions.

Ransom seems in the stream of speculation where Winters stands on the banks of assertion. As to who is right, I would say both are, partly. It is the old problem of the one and the many. As to who is more prudent, I would say Ransom is, because he realizes his own fallibility, that finite being is in time. It seems to me that the critic by the intense energy of his mind MUST come to conclusions, but always be willing to let these conclusions evolve, if there seems sufficient reason for evolvement. By evolvement here I mean change, but especially developmental change. Critics may never rest at the breast of infantile security but should always be willing to move out through the darkness and into the maturity of groping speculation.

Ransom is OPERATIONALLY Aristotelian, DISPOSITIONALLY nominalistic and relativistic[95] but this very relativism gives him an openness that Winters does not seem to possess.

I have tried in this chapter to give the reader a sense of Ransom's substance as a critic, a sense of his disposition, his convictions, his influences, and his critical and philosophical orientation. In later chapters, I hope to go more fully into the flowering of this critical stem as it blooms in Ransom's critical texts. Ransom is an ontological particularist because he is consumed with a love and interest in the 'world's body', and he doubts all else but its existence.

---

[95] In "Wam for Maw: Dogma versus Discursiveness in Criticism", *Sewanee Review*, XLIX (Oct., 1941), 520–36, W. S. Knickerbocker lists fourteen variations of Ransom's definition of poetry that appear in *The New Criticism*. Winters would never be guilty of this multiplicity.

III

THE MATERIAL OBJECT, THE CAUSE
AND THE NATURE OF THE POEM

In this study and in this chapter, the movement is from the universal to the particular, a movement corresponding to Ransom's thinking in "The Concrete Universal: Observations on the Understanding of Poetry"[1] (1955). There he thinks first of the universal, then of the moral universal and, lastly, of the concrete universal which is the poem. Aristotle long ago urged us to know the causes of things in order to know their nature, and so we shall. By knowing the cause of the poem, which in 1955 had become for Ransom 'the moral universal', we shall get to the nature and the objects of the poem.

A. EVOLUTION TOWARDS HUMAN IMMANENCY IN RANSOM'S
REALIZATION OF THE 'STUFF' OF POETRY

Ransom's notion of the 'material cause' or the material objects of the poem developed from the time of *The New Criticism* to his pivotal essay on the 'concrete universal'. This has been partially indicated in the previous chapter. In "The Concrete Universal: Observations on the Understanding of Poetry", (1955), Ransom is no longer preoccupied with the intimations of the 'beloved objects'. He has become more concerned with the Kantian synchronization of the mind with reality. He has become interested in the poet's psychology as concretely embodied in the poem, instead of the poet's imitation of a beloved object outside himself. It is a question of developing emphasis, not of exclusion. It seems that the earlier emphasis was less tenable because it emphasized exterior reality to the detriment of interior reality and emphasized,

[1] *Poems and Essays*, pp. 159–85.

perhaps, too heavily, the nature of the objects as 'beloved' or precious. For one might ask, "Is poetry merely a question of man's discovering a reality outside himself or dynamically realizing himself in relation to and participating in existence?" Ransom's early emphasis in this respect reminds one of Aristotle's emphasis in the *Poetics:* from an aesthetic point of view there is too much thinking about outward action and other-than-self reality and too little thinking of inward action and reality as self. Although Aristotle knows well that action follows existence he rarely alludes to action as a manifestation of immanency "for tragedy is an imitation not of men, but of an action and of life and life consists in action and its end is a mode of action, not of quality . . . and on actions all success or failure depends."[2] We cannot help thinking that Aristotle would have been impatient or amazed at Hamlet's soliloquies and Macbeth's cerebral rummagings, and at the fleshly beauty of the diction (which he puts last, when talking of poetry!) in *Antony and Cleopatra*. When he speaks of the cause of poetry as being a natural instinct for imitation, he often thinks of the objects of imitation in terms of exterior and otherness instead of man contending with himself and responding to the impress of existence. Aristotle's biological tunic shows through his aesthetic toga. Aesthetics and criticism have developed since Aristotle, and Ransom has developed since *The New Criticism* and *The World's Body* because of his realization of self: self as artist, and self as an object to be poetically configured. This is the emphasis of the existentialists[3] and of Freud, both of whom have influenced the world and Ransom. These and other thinkers have realized that man is in a process of developing awareness of self. And Ransom has been borne along with this emphasis in his notion of the concrete universal: man's awareness realized in the poetic body of words. The concrete universal is the result of man realizing himself in the world and responding to the world.

Ransom's earlier notion of the object of art as 'beloved', may surprise one a little because it seems restricted in vision and somewhat naive. He meant beloved as precious or familiar; he did not mean what W. H. Auden means by 'sacred' in "Making, Knowing

[2] Aristotle, *The Poetics, The Basic Works of Aristotle*, ed. Richard McKeon (New York, 1941), p. 1461.

[3] See "Poetry: II, The Final Cause", *Kenyon Review*, IX (Autumn, 1947), 644ff.

and Judging".[4] Auden's sacred objects are those that draw the
attention of the primary imagination. They put the poet in awe,
despite himself. They are not necessarily loved. "A sacred being
may be attractive or repulsive—a swan or octopus—beautiful or
ugly—toothless hag or a fair young child—good or evil . . ."[5]
Ransom's object was something sought for the sake of itself, something wished to be more fully discovered because loved: a pair of
gloves, a little girl, a walking stick, a certain tree, and so on. But
are there not too many poems which have to do with agony and
despair and loss to have one accept Ransom's propositions about
these 'precious objects' as the object of the poem? It is a valuable
insight but can it be taken as a valid, universal hypothesis for the
creation of the poem? Hopkins' darkness is something that one
never wants to undergo, and Iago is not a 'precious object'.

B. THE CAUSE OF THE POEM: THE MORAL AND
CONCRETE UNIVERSALS

Ransom has developed to include in his notion of the poem more
than the precious objects. He has more recently been concerned
with the 'concrete universal', with a realization or a foreconceit
or a universal given act by verbalized matter. Although Hegel was
the originator of the term 'concrete universal', Ransom cannot
follow him, for Hegel has abandoned art in abandoning nature.
For Ransom, Hegel thinks that man no longer needs nature to
complete his realization of existence. Man's universal is complete
and full-blown in itself and needs only to be applied to the world
to organize it. The mind of man no longer passes through the
world seeking for answers but applies its realized inner order to
the world, especially to politics, sociology,[6] and other practical
realms. Hegel is 'benign' but too 'aggressive' for Ransom; he is
an ideational ruffian,[7] who wishes to superimpose his idea upon
the spontaneity of the world. Hegel's mind is too much of a strait
jacket for Ransom's world and Ransom's poetry. Therefore Ransom
moves to Kant, who has a far more understanding notion of the

[4] W. H. Auden, *The Dyer's Hand* (New York, 1962), pp. 51–60.
[5] *Ibid.*, p. 55.
[6] "The Concrete Universal", *Poems and Essays*, pp. 167–69.
[7] *Ibid.*, p. 167.

relation of human existence to nature[8] (that phenomenon which is other than self and is usually realized as concrete). Nature for Kant was not simple but dense and manifold, with its tissue of accretions and intricate unfoldings. Kant did not think that man could afford to be aggressive in his attempt to know and use the world; he must gradually and delicately realize a certain ontological sympathy between two realities: man and nature. The beautiful, for example, was neither a product of man's mind or of nature, but man realizing nature. The ordering and the making of things must be done delicately and cautiously in order not to destroy the spontaneity and dissolve the authenticity of the knowledge gained. This, it seems, is close to what Ransom thinks of Kant. Ransom sees Kant thinking of man as one who is blind and who will come to see only if he handles objects thoroughly, gently, and with a cautious respect. For example, if one were blind and wanted to know what a freshly-made clay statue looked like, he would not do it by firmly gripping the face with his hands. That would distort and destroy the original contour. He would 'sympathetically' and gently feel his way along the contours of the statue until he realized the configured existence of the statue and he would fulfill himself in the realization of its beauty.

Let us pass now to the result of Kant's influence on Ransom: the Universal and its types, and under what conditions they are found in poetry. As mentioned above, there are three species of universal for Ransom: the pure universal, the moral universal, and the concrete universal.[9] The 'pure' universal is a conception in the mind of man; Ransom explains this Hegelian species of universal this way: "any idea of the mind which proposes a little universe, or organized working combinations of parts, where there is a whole and a single effect to be produced, and the heterogeneous parts must perform their several duties faithfully in order to bring it about."[10] But where Hegel would have complete confidence in the self-sufficiency—the integrity—of the universal, Ransom and Kant would be more cautious and would realize that man needs the world to give the universal its existential adjustment. The mind, and, thus, the human idea is not divine or infallible for Ransom and cannot be expected to fit perfectly into its worldly

[8] *Ibid.*, pp. 169–70.
[9] *Ibid.*, pp. 163–66.
[10] *Ibid.*, p. 163.

slot, or 'organize' perfectly, what it preconceives. There is the world's unpredictability and phenomenal mystery which must be gently adjusted to man's preconception and will always overflow this preconception.

Next, we have the concrete universal. For Ransom, it is the objective realization of the 'Pure' universal in matter. The concrete universal has two essential ramifications: the SCIENTIFIC and the MORAL. The scientific concrete universal is a PREDATORY universal; it has a practical end in mind and it will make exacting demands upon nature in order to fulfill its end. The scientific universal is concerned with nature not as an end, but as a means. And its matter will always perfectly EXHAUST its form or universal.

Ransom says:

Science means to have its Concrete Universal just right, and has it so; and the crucial factor in getting it right would perhaps be the determination of the scientist, if he does not find the right parts already existing in the state of nature, to alter the materials he does find, til [sic] they become right; to compound them or purify them, grow them or manufacture them, fit them to size and shape, and so on; in the Universal as designed there are specifications which they must meet. So the parts of the finished Concrete Universal do have their logical blueprint perfection as follows: Not one necessary part missing; nor one unnecessary part showing; nor a part showing which is either excessive or deficient in its action even though some one might be (by the carelessness of the designer, or the stubbornness of the material), and still not fail to do its work after a fashion.[11]

The bridge-maker's matter must absolutely conform to his blueprint. If not, the bridge will crumble and people will be killed. The bridge-maker forces his universal upon the world for the sake of human transportation and money in his pocket.

On the other hand, the MORAL concrete universal has more to do with man's realization of self. It transcends, in its purpose, the fulfillment of man's organic, appetitive needs. It has more to do with the understanding of the order and purpose in existence, as ends in themselves, and less to do with using this order and purpose as means for material accomplishment. The moral universal is begotten of the high, aspirational regions of man. It considers man in his metaphysical and ultimate relations to existence, and it is found most authentically existing in art and specifically in the

[11] *Ibid.*, p. 164.

poem. Thus, "the universal of the poem is a moral universal".[12] But even with the poetic moral universal, we have degrees of authenticity. The least authentic poem is that which explicitly sets before us the way in which we should ACT. The poet may here use a hero as an exemplar of human action. This is the only type of poetry which Plato applauds in the tenth book of *The Republic*. And, according to Ransom's explanations, it would seem that poems which are baldly didactic, such as Pope's "Essay on Criticism" and Edward Young's "Night Thoughts", romantic poetry such as Longfellow's "Psalm of Life", Emerson's "Give All to Love", Whittier's "Massachusetts to Virginia" might be included here. Ransom might not agree with all these selections, but these do seem to fall within that class of poetry which is baldly directive in its lines.

On a slightly higher level of non-authenticity would be that type of poetry which does not direct us how to act but how to think, how to make the right choice in order to act well. Again, Pope's "Essay on Criticism" or "Essay on Man" might fit here. So, also, would other poems of the authors mentioned just above. Ransom succinctly describes what he means by this second type of poetry:

> A little less disreputable (less absurdly simple) would be a kind of poetry given to representing moral situations where it is difficult not so much to do one's duty, but to know just which among the several possibilities is the duty one must do; exemplary in its practical judgments, in the nicety of its distinction among the moral ideas. Here we come close to Hegel's weakness and, by the same token, to Hegel's strength. But still this is not poetry as Kant conceives it consistently, or as Hegel conceives it ideally.[13]

To the extent that the poet becomes a 'moral tailor', Ransom disowns him. For the tailor cuts his matter exactly to fit his blueprint. He is not a discoverer, he does not realize himself more fully for knowing the world, but he has cut the world to the size of his mind. The poet must be a voyager, a seeker who realizes the world as his dynamic and spontaneous complement, and about which he is never sure. The world is the unpredictable spouse of the poet, through whom the poet comes to know the myriad recesses of his own personality and psychic potentialities. He never superimposes his private morality, his private moral universal upon nature but lets nature engage and, if he is lucky, symbolize his moral universal.

[12] *Ibid.*, p. 165.
[13] *Ibid.*, p. 166.

Ransom gives an example of what he means by true aesthetical balance in the process of creation when he rephrases Kant's example of the landscape gardener in his garden.[14] Kant's gardener has a universal of what he wants the garden to look like, but despite this universal and beneath this universal there is the free, intricate play of nature — the tissues of natural irrelevancy that escape the form of the gardener's universal, and yet give it the recalcitrant spontaneity to make it art. "Nature seems to have no inclination to reject or even to resent the human Universal, for now obtains the condition of 'freedom under law', and its consequence of beauty."[15]

The poet cannot and must not try to determine nature, for he is not the exemplar cause of nature. Nature subsists outside himself and is not really under his control; yet it will offer itself to the poet's imagination in order that he may concretize an idea, if the poet is not too procrustean in his demands.

Let us examine some examples of authentic and non-authentic poetic embodiments of the moral universal, moral universals which have either poetically aborted or have been authentically born in the flesh of nature and time.

The first example that Ransom gives of an aborted universal is from Browning's "Pippa Passes":

> The year's at the spring
> And day's at the morn;
> Morning's at seven;
> The hill-side's dew pearled;
> The lark's on the wing;
> The snail's on the thorn:
> God's in his heaven —
> All's right with the world.[16]

Ransom thinks that the first six lines of this passage are an effective concretization of Pippa's joy at being alive in the world. But the last two lines abort. The poem becomes much too ulterior in motive, here, in its non-incarnated and disproportionate statement of fact. This is merely a moral tag, without sufficient justification for its existence. Browning is trying to bring us to his moral universal without an aesthetic reason. This is bad art because it does

[14] *Ibid.*, pp. 171–72.
[15] *Ibid.*, p. 171.
[16] *Ibid.*, p. 172.

not have the gentle, subtle finesse needed to objectify or concretize its universal.

Ransom offers another example of where the moral universal shows nakedly without its 'manifold of sense' or verbalized flesh. It is "Bermudas" by Marvell. Ransom says:

> He [Marvell] is more direct than metaphorical in "Bermudas" where the colonists recite the kindness of the natural element which God has given them.

> He gave us this eternal spring,
> Which here enamels everything;
> And sends the fowls to us in care,
> On daily visits through the air.
> He hangs in shades the orange bright,
> Like golden lamps in a green night.
> And does in the pomgranates close
> Jewels more rich than Ormus shows.
> He makes the figs our mouths to meet;
> And throws the melons at our feet.
> But apples plants of such a price,
> No tree could ever bear them twice.
> With cedars, chosen by his hand,
> From Lebanon, he stores the land,
> And makes the hollow seas that roar,
> Proclaim the ambergris on shore.
> He cast (of which we rather boast)
> The gospels pearl upon our coast.
> And in these rocks for us did frame
> A temple, where to sound his name.

> The purpose of nature is identified completely with the care of Providence. Kant would not have found it according to the canon. The best we can say of it is that the colonists sing this naive song as they row their boat, so that there is drama in it.[17]

This poem is too ideal and too direct for Ransom. He would rather have the reader conclude for himself, by means of a 'concrete universal' in the poem, what is Marvell's moral universal than to have the colonists recite a lesson to him. It is up to the inter-play of the understanding and the imagination to incarnate the universal so that it does not create aesthetical 'distaste' in the mind of the reader. The poet must give incarnate universals for incarnate readers.

---

[17] *Ibid.*, pp. 176–77.

Yet, Ransom does not exclude all poems whose moral universal shows. In fact, he says "it would be wrong to give the impression that in the poem, necessarily, the intellectual universal has always disappeared from sight and now exists only in the concrete. It is my impression that as often as not, a poem will recite its two versions side by side."[18] He gives an example of this duality in Portia's speaking of mercy in the trial of Antonio. "The quality of mercy is not strained", is her moral universal and "It droppeth as the gentle rain from heaven upon the place beneath", is her concretization of the universal. Does Ransom, here, contradict himself? Must the universal be submerged or not? If not, how may it not be submerged and still be an authentic poem? This problem is confusing, and his standards of judgment sometimes seem to be arbitrary. But let us compare the Pippa passage with Portia's and see why he will accept one and not the other. In Pippa's passage there seems to be an abruptness, a non-consonance between the tenor and the vehicle. Do the spring of the year, and the morning of the day, the time of the day, the dew, the lark's song, the snail on the thorn evoke an affirmation of the existence of God and the order of the world in the reader's mind? Or does the writer too rudely force the moral universal into the reader's mind? Taking it as the verbalized culmination of Pippa's joy, I think the passage is justified, but taking the first six lines as an objective correlative to the last two, the passage does seem to have some abruptness. This baldness, this lack of adequate comparison may be what Ransom objects to.

In the Portia passage, there is a more consonant transition from tenor to vehicle. It does not wrench the reader's mind to pass from 'a quality not strained' to the falling of dew. The universal of the poet and the object of nature are more synthesized—more 'sympathetic' to each other. This seems to be the significance of these two examples given by Ransom. Tags are not allowed; organically developed comparisons are.

Lines that might completely abort, for Ransom, would be Tennyson's last stanza of "In Memoriam":

> That God, which ever lives and loves,
> One God, one law, one element,

18 *Ibid.*, p. 174.

> And one far-off divine event,
> To which the whole creation moves.[19]

Ransom has little patience with this sort of moral didacticism. The poet is not here a discoverer, not an ontologist, not a searcher; he is a promulgator; he is a pragmatist who rudely forces his moral universal upon us without sufficient poetic justification. He has not given us a sufficient foundation to evoke the emotion or the human affect that he wishes. There is no pervading comparison, no natural correlative that causes the emotion in us that rises up in the poet. This is oratory with poetic pretence. Poetry is not reducible to sheer moral discourse. Ransom was even more vehement about this when he made his distinction between prose and poetry in *The New Criticism:*

> At any rate, a moral content is a kind of content which has been suggested as the peculiar content of poetry, and it does not work; it is not really peculiar to poetry but perfectly available for prose; besides, it is not the content of a great deal of poetry. I suggest that the differentia of poetry as discourse is an ontological one. It treats an order of existence, a grade of objectivity, which cannot be treated in scientific discourse.

> This should not prove unintelligible. We live in a world which must be distinguished from the world, or the worlds, for there are many of them, which we treat in our scientic discourses. They are its reduced, emasculated, and docile versions. Poetry intends to recover the denser and more refractory original world which we know loosely through our perceptions and memories. By this supposition it is a kind of knowledge which is radically or ontologically distinct.[20]

Ransom does not like Marvell's "Bermudas", for the same general reason; it is too direct—its moral universal has not been corporealized by a metaphor or a simile derived from the body of this world. Ransom does not like his worlds confused. He does not like the poet's theology or practical morality getting between the reader and his apprehension of literature and the world. He does not like theological begging of the question in terms of the poem. He is distrustful of those people who drag in God,[21] because

---

[19] Alfred Tennyson, *The Poetical Works of Alfred Tennyson* (Chicago, 1895), p. 503.

[20] "Wanted: An Ontological Critic", *The New Criticism*, p. 281.

[21] T. E. Hulme is also distrustful of people who are preoccupied with the infinite in their poetry, though for different reasons. See "Romanticism and

they want to promulgate a way of security in terms of their own complacency. Rather, the poet's theology is always tentative and searching, and in terms of THIS world. It is a product of the 'negative capability' of Keats. The poet has the uncertainty of a human being, and therefore should write humanly, that is uncertainly, analogously, and metaphorically. "To the theologian, the poet might want to say 'one world at a time.' "[22]

C. THE MOST APPROPRIATE CONCRETE UNIVERSAL: THE METAPHOR

Though Ransom will accept a synchronized existence of the abstract and the embodied universal in the same poem, it seems that he prefers the universal to be totally embodied in words, especially in metaphor. Metaphor is the most complete, most whole and most consonant way of incarnating the universal.

To say "metaphor" tirelessly, with brutal repetition, is one militant way of defending nature as the element to which the Universal is referred, and therefore the element to which poetry has to look. I think the defenders of poetry would not mind saying that they are not prepared to abandon nature, because that would be the abandonment of metaphor, which, in turn would mean the abandonment of poetry; which, when they have weighed it, would be a serious abridgment of the range of human experience.[23]

And what does metaphor mean for Ransom? He explains its meaning this way: " . . . the way of the imagination in giving objective or Concrete existence to the homeless moral universal . . . it would seem a decisive word for his [Kant's] understanding of poetry; it gives us the sense of nature accepting the universal readily into its infinite system, and lending to it what metaphysical sanction is possible."[24]

Classicism", *Speculations*, 2nd ed. (New York and London, 1936), pp. 120, 128. In partial response to both objections I should say "Let no man dictate another's experience. The domain of poetry is existence, real or hallucinatory."

[22] The Concrete Universal", *Poems and Essays*, p. 184.

[23] *Ibid.*, p. 181.

[24] *Ibid.*, pp. 181–2.

1. *Metaphorical Knowledge and Psychic Harmony: Ransom Versus Richards*

It is in reference to the poet's metaphorical knowledge of this world that Ransom attacked Richards' distinction between pseudo and scientific statements. For Richards, in his *Principles of Literary Criticism* (1924), the poet creates an harmonic whole of pseudo-statements, statements with no real referent value, in order to create a harmony of multiple interests in himself and, perhaps, in the reader. Richards believes in 1924 that the end of the poem is the behavioristic reconciliation of psychic opposites. As music and some modern painting have no ideational reference to reality, so the poem need not. It may only organize the stimuli and the interests of man's inner world. It may give psychic tranquility by aesthetic form. But to Ransom this poetic non-reference is really inconceivable. If there is no reference to some objective and commonly known existence, then there is no intelligibility. Man has an INTER-EST in existence; he responds to existence which other men participate in, and he has a nature which others possess. Ransom responds tersely, in defense of poetic truth: "Inter-esse means to be environed, and interest means sensitiveness to environment. To be interested is to try to gain cognition, to do what Mr. Richards wickedly denies to poetic experience and grants exclusively to science: to seek the truth. I think the biologist would justify only this conception of the function of our interests."[25] To define poetry and its ends in terms of psychic harmony and affective response seems, for Ransom, to lead to critical nihilism. There must be some objective reference to which the critic, the poet, and the reader can appeal, so that they may truly judge, communicate, and understand the poetic statement. How shall the critic understand an emotional attitude —its legitimacy and its maturity— if he cannot imagine himself in a concrete circumstance to which an attitude has reference? On what basis shall a critic judge an attitude, if the subject of the attitude does not exist or cannot be understood? Ransom demands the emotion's anchorage in the world of concrete reference. We see in the following passage that he is a close reader of T. S. Eliot —especially Eliot's essay "Hamlet

[25] "A Psychologist Looks at Poetry", *The World's Body*, p. 155. See also Ransom's notion of the poem and the poet's function in "Criticism Inc.", *The World's Body*, p. 348.

and his Problems",[26] where Eliot speaks of the 'objective correlative'.

The expert and most characteristic method employed by a poet for communicating feelings is said to be the device of metaphor. But, we must remark once more, no feeling is identified by a metaphor until an objective situation has been identified by it. In short, the one automatic and sure method of identifying a feeling is to furnish an objective situation and say: Now imagine your feeling in this situation. Under these circumstances I do not see why the critic needs to do more than talk about the objective situations. The feelings will be their strict correlatives and the pursuit of the feelings will be gratuitous.

In this connection it will be interesting to look at Richards' remarks on Sentimentality. For him, a sentimental reader is a person too facile, or too copious, in his affective responses to the object; his show of affections (as in those protocols which were "gushing") seems to exceed the occasion. But this must mean that it exceeds the objective occasion which is the "communicated" one. He is adding out of his own imagination to the occasion, or in his lack of experience he is misconstruing it; his reading is off the text. A sentimental poet, similarly, must be the poet who neglects the complete communication of his occasion, and for a short-cut pronounces the affective words that the reader should pronounce for himself, and then only on the understanding that they were appropriate to a communication that had been received. Whether of reader or poet, the error seems to reduce to Richards' idea of Stock Response: the affective activity is not grounded in precise cognition.

Richards always holds this—though in later books he will stop reiterating it—that the heart of the aesthetic experience is the affective activity. One of the considerations which seem to me to have had weight in driving him to this dogma is his failure to find any objective correlative for the sense of "beauty".[27]

Knowledge of the world, though a personal knowledge, not verbal therapeutics, is the end of poetry for Ransom. "An account of poetry as knowledge by images, reporting the fulness of particularity", says Ransom, "would hardly be acceptable to Mr. Richards."[28]

---

[26] *Selected Essays* (New York, 1950), pp. 124–25.

[27] "I. A. Richards: The Psychological Critic", *The New Criticism*, pp. 50–51; in this passage Ransom directs his attention to Richards' "Irrelevant Associations and Stock Responses", Pt. III, ch. 5, *Practical Criticism* (London, 1929).

[28] "A Psychologist Looks at Poetry", *The World's Body*, p. 158; for an attack on Ransom's 'poetry as knowledge' theory, see Lee T. Lemon, *The Partial Critics* (New York, 1965), pp. 99–106.

Ransom believes that the emotions have a place in the poem, but they are a shifting basis for discussion about the poem. He is concerned with the concrete, poetic representation which will spontaneously elicit correlative emotions in the reader and which have given rise to the emotions of the poet. "The affections are involved by the poem", says Ransom, "but the important thing for theory to see is that they attach spontaneously to the items of the context. And since they attach spontaneously, they scarcely need to enter into critical discussion. We need only to say that the poem develops its local particularities while it progresses towards its functional completion."[29]

2. Poetic Dualism and Poetic Unity:
Ransom versus Brooks

Though Ransom believes that the most accurate and natural poetic means for the poet to embody his notion of the world by the world itself is the metaphor, he will not THEORETICALLY admit that the metaphor can be the whole poem or that the attitude embodied in the metaphor can be its unity. And here is where Brooks challenges Ransom. On the one hand, Ransom PRACTICALLY likes the complete submergence of the poet's universal in the flesh of words; on the other hand, he theoretically holds for the poem's ideational 'core' or 'logic' as against 'tissue of meaning' or metaphor. This oscillation and confusion in Ransom's criticism cannot be resolved, but only explained. And perhaps by this explanation Ransom's oscillation may become somewhat of a dialectic to the reader. In this regard, let us first consider what Ransom means by the word 'logic' above. Sometimes he means primarily progression, as when he says:

If the poem has to be defended in the wholeness of its being, what of that character in the poem which makes it discourse? In whatever terms, the poem has generality and definition, if anybody wants them; it remains, if the grammarian looks at it, a species of Aristotelian discourse. Thus it has a beginning, middle and an end if the argument is sizable enough to bother about such things; and otherwise there is the "point" of the poem, the act of prediction, or the sheer core object, with such qualifications as may appear; and everywhere that minute kind of order which we call syntax, not fatally overlaid or concealed. To so much logical formalism the meta-

---

[29] "The Psychological Critic", *The New Criticism*, p. 58.

phors and brilliances have to adapt, and surely it is very advantageous for them.[30]

At the other times, he means the WHAT of discursive argument in contrast to the HOW, as when he talks of the logical structure 'with its meaning texture',[31] when he writes of an 'abstract from history',[32] or, as seen above, when he refers to an 'act of predication'. Perhaps he is trying to write the HOW and the WHAT into one discursive term, for sometimes he uses the word 'argument', which implies both the HOW and the WHAT of discursive discourse.

Often, and perhaps usually, we are able to take much pride in the mere paraphrase or argument of the poem, by itself; yet the paraphrase is a fair version of the logical structure. The "arguments" of poems are apt to seem rather commonplace. They have as a rule less distinction, than the prose arguments that are able to stand by themselves; and they are not meant to stand by themselves. The arguments are for the sake of the poems; without the arguments there can be no poems.[33]

But where does this leave a poet's existential realization or epiphany of some nuance of existence? Must the lyric poet have a meter-making argument? Do the terms 'logical core' or 'prose discourse' have a certain inadequacy, for the poem really has no prose discourse? One may generalize about a poetic experience, but is this the poem? In regard to this problem, Ransom may be too dualistic to be critically right, for he seems to transform a possible distinction into an impossible separation, and seems to confuse a syllogistic with a poetic experience and creation. This dualism of Ransom's is exemplified in his comments on the critical theories of Cleanth Brooks.

At this point, I would propose a certain wide and overall conception of the poem. A little while ago I was urging Brooks to acknowledge the logical form of the poem as something fixed and—for the hard-headed English-speaking public—invincible; which the showy metaphors, episodic or "dominant" as they may be, had better make their peace with, especially since it would do them no harm; and I had the idea of a poem as a great "paradox", a construct looking two ways, with the logic trying to dominate

---

[30] "Why Critics Don't Go Mad", *Poems and Essays*, p. 150.

[31] "Yvor Winters: The Logical Critic", *The New Criticism*, p. 260.

[32] "I. A. Richards: The Psychological Critic", *The New Criticism*, p. 114.

[33] "The Logical Critic", p. 269.

the metaphors, and the metaphors trying to dominate the logic, and neither or both (as we have it in paradoxes), succeeding.[34]

Cleanth Brooks, in contrast to Ransom's concern for logical coherency, theorizes that the poem coheres through a pervading attitude that is given verbal life by a dominant metaphor. The unity of the poem will be in attitudinal direction rather than in logical progression. In respect to this problem of unity and how it is poetically achieved, Brooks says this:

> But to deny that the coherence of a poem is reflected in a logical para-phrase of its "real meaning" is not, of course, to deny the coherence of poetry; it is rather to assert that its coherence is to be sought elsewhere. The charac-teristic unity of a poem (even of those poems which may accidentally possess a logical unity as well as this poetic unity) lies in the unification of attitudes into a hierarchy subordinated to a local and governing attitude. In the uni-fied poem, the poet "has come to terms" with his experience. This does not merely eventuate in a logical conclusion. The conclusion of the poem is the working out of various tensions — set up by whatever means — by proposi-tions, metaphors, symbols. The unity is achieved by a dramatic process, not a logical; it represents an equilibrium of forces, not a formula. It is "proved" as a dramatic conclusion is proved: by its ability to resolve the conflicts which have been accepted as the données of the drama.[35]

Coherency and unity for Brooks are in the attitude as embodied in the dominant metaphor. And this metaphor is not paraphrasable, because of its necessity to exist as metaphor. In respect to this problem, Brooks gives the example of an English teacher struggling in class to paraphrase a poem. After a great while the teacher is able to approximate the poem, but this very approximation is done in terms of symbols and metaphors, not in terms of logic and denotative progression. The look, the gesture and the emotion of the teacher have come to bear in his explanation. In fact, the teacher has had to escape logic in order to get at the poem.[36]

In Ransom's essay "Shakespeare at Sonnets",[37] there is further evidence of ambiguity in Ransom's critical language, and of further

[34] "Why Critics Don't Go Mad", *Poems and Essays*, p. 157; concerning the 'prose discourse' of the poem, see also "Inorganic Muses", *Kenyon Review*, IV (Autumn, 1942), 406–7.

[35] Cleanth Brooks, *The Well-Wrought Urn* (New York, 1947), pp. 206–7.

[36] *Ibid.*, footnote 1, p. 206; concerning this problem of unity and the means to achieve it, see also Ransom's review, "Cleanth Brooks, *Modern Poetry and the Tradition*", *Kenyon Review*, II (Spring, 1940), 247–51. Here Ransom deplores the lack of logical firmness in poetry.

[37] *The World's Body*, pp. 270–304.

difference between the critical theories of Cleanth Brooks and
John Crowe Ransom. These two critics do not make the same
demands upon the metaphor in the poetic text. In this essay,
metaphor takes on the qualities of logic for Ransom. There is no
'construct looking two ways' here, no tension between logic and metaphor, for metapher has become the logic. There must be, for Ransom, one single development of the metaphorical premise; it may not
be poetically splintered. The directive principle of the metaphor has
become, here, the directive mental power of the poet's intellect.
The metaphor in this essay is the adequate objective form for the
emotions of the poet. And in the consistent and progressive development of this metaphor will the reader cognitively understand
the emotions of the poet. Brooks, however, would not give the
metaphor the function of logic. The dominant metaphor would
still be the poetic correlative for the poet's dominant attitude
towards a nuance of existence. The metaphors or comparisons in
the poem need not have the rigid intellectual development de-
manded by Ransom. In this essay, Ransom expects that the
emotion be given an intellective poetic face. Brooks would prefer
that the poetic face of the poem be a correlative to the human
experience, which is a unity, not a duality, of emotion and intel-
lection. Brooks will allow emotive meanderings in the poem as long
as they reinforce the dominant tone and attitude in the poem.

It is because Shakespeare does not give the metaphors of his
sonnets progressive and consistent development that Ransom
criticizes him. Shakespeare moves 'associatively', 'psychologically',
but not logically;[38] his metaphors do not give a sequential, logical
wholeness to many of his sonnets. "Structurally, Shakespeare is
a careless workman"[39] and he writes 'a poetry of wonderful im-
precision';[40] his poems do not evidence the hard-wrought form
and consistently developed conceits of the metaphysical Donne.
Ransom develops what he means by a metaphysical quality in
poetry, a quality that Shakespeare does not substantially possess
in his sonnets:

The impulse to metaphysical poetry, I shall assume, consists in com-
mitting the feelings in the case—those of unrequited love for example—to
their determination within the elected figure. But Shakespeare was rarely

[38] "Shakespeare at Sonnets", *The World's Body*, pp. 284, 289 and 302.
[39] *Ibid.*, p. 278.
[40] *Ibid.*, p. 281.

willing to abandon his feelings to this fate, which is another way of saying that he would not risk the consequences of his own imagination. He censored these consequences, to give them sweetness, to give them even dignity; he would go a little way with one figure, usually a reputable one, then anticipate the consequences, or the best of them, and take up another figure.[41]

Donne, however, is the supreme architect of the lyric in English because he is able to give a complete cognitive unity to his poems by performing supremely the mental task of controlling the life of the imagination.

The evidence of this cognitive control is the test which the critic must have in mind when evaluating the poem. The cognition, the 'logic',[42] is the bone structure of the poem, and in reference to this stable structure the critic should judge the beauty and the worth of the poem. Ransom does not like his emotion and cognition mixed in an 'association of sensibility',[43] either in criticism or in poetry. This association leads to 'associative' poetry, which is amorphous poetry. The cognition in the poem is the hard, stable element which is receptive of poetic criticism. In the process of contrasting Shakespeare's Sonnet LV to Donne's "Valediction: Of The Booke", Ransom spells out why he thinks Donne is superior to Shakespeare as a lyric poet. He begins by commenting on Shakespeare's sonnet:

It is a "strong" sonnet, not quite intelligent enough to be metaphysical. It begins,

> Not marble, nor the gilded monuments
> Of princes shall [sic] outlive his powerful rime,

yet what it develops is not the circumstantial immortality of the rime, and the beloved inhabiting it, but the mortality of the common marbles

---

[41] *Ibid.*, pp. 286–7.

[42] By the words 'cognitive', 'logical', and 'objective' Ransom wishes to denote the power and the effect of the mind as opposed to the amorphous power and effect of the emotions, which, in themselves, cannot be the subject of literary criticism. By 'cognitive', in this essay, he means MENTAL, as opposed to emotional; by 'logical', he means the PROGRESSION of the mental power in words, and by 'objective' he means the hard, STABLE EFFECT of the mental power in words.

We are confronted here with a difficulty which often faces the reader of Ransom's essays: the partial ambiguity of his language. In an attempt, probably, to escape the jargon of philosophical language, his use of words has become too flexible.

[43] T. S. Eliot, "The Metaphysical Poets", *Selected Essays*, pp. 246–7.

and monuments, an old story with Shakespeare, and as to the immortality makes the single effort:

> 'Gainst death and all oblivious enmity
> Shall you pace forth.[44]

Ransom thinks that Shakespeare does not develop the poetic figure contained in the first couplet. The immortality of the rime and the beloved preserved in it have not been poetically developed. Shakespeare's imagination has not been sufficiently directed by his intellect. Instead of specifying, in an objective and logical fashion, how the beloved will be preserved in his poems, he shifts his imaginative ground and concerns himself with the mortality of marbles and monuments. For Ransom, this is partly 'associative' poetry[45] whose directive forces are blind forces: the imagination and the emotions are unable to give intelligible form and sequential progression to a poem; they need the sight and focus of the mind, the intellect or the cognitive powers—terms which Ransom uses interchangeably. It is because of this impulsive or shifting blindness that Ransom has a distaste for Romantic poetry, which he identifies, in this essay, with 'associative' poetry. To this associative poetry he opposes 'behavioristic' or 'metaphysical' poetry.[46] The "metaphysical poets", he says, "are selfconscious and deliberate, and in fact like technical psychologists. They start with the feelings, they objectify these imaginatively [under the power of the mind] into external action. They think that poetry, just as behavioristic psychologists think that psychology, can make nothing out of the feelings as they stand."[47]

In contrast to the associationist Shakespeare, he cites how the behaviorist Donne objectifies his feelings into a poetic figure. I quote the poem "Valediction: Of The Booke", as Ransom quotes it, and follow with his comment.

> This Booke, as long-lived as the elements,
> Or as the world's forme, this all-graved tome

[44] "Shakespeare at Sonnets", *The World's Body*, p. 287.

[45] *Ibid.*, p. 291. In his essay "Unconscious Expectations in the Reading of Poetry", *English Literary History*, IX (Dec., 1942), 243–44, M. H. Abrams says that Ransom reads Shakespeare through the eyes of Donne.

[46] *Ibid.* For an interesting and adverse comment on Ransom's opposition to romantic, 'associative' poetry see Richard H. Fogle, "Romantic Bards and Metaphysical Reviewers", *English Literary History*, XII (Sept,. 1945), 221–50. See especially pp. 231–33.

[47] *Ibid.*, pp. 291–2.

In cypher writ, or new made Idiome
(We for love's clergie only are instruments), —
When this booke is made thus,
Should again the ravenous
Vandals and Gauls inundate us,
Learning were safe; in this our universe
Schooles might learn Sciences, Spheres Musick,
      Angeles Verse.

One understands that he really means what he says: a book. In the three
stanzas following he shows respectively what the Divines, the Lawyers, and
the Statesmen will learn from this book, and in a final stanza returns to relate
to a lover's absence the labor of compiling it.[48]

Ransom concludes his commentary on the two poems by pointing
out that it is the business of literary theorists to direct their attention to what is objective in the poem — to what has been sufficiently
crystallized in images, under the power of the intellect, to be
cognitively digestible. Ransom insists on the hard, logical development of the metaphorical premise. Without this development there
is no real criticism, for there is no really intelligible poem.

Cleanth Brooks, again in contrast to Ransom, does not think
that the metaphor needs to be married to logical progression or
tailored to the 'prose line of argument'. The poem may have its
associative 'meanderings', as long as these meanderings strengthen
the central attitude of the poem. It is therefore not the logic or
even the consistent development of metaphor that gives the poem
its central strength for Brooks, but the force of its tone and attitude.
Brooks develops his argument in this fashion.

But the meanderings of a good poem (they are meanderings only from
the standpoint of the prose paraphrase of the poem) are not negative, and
they do not have to be excused; and most of all, we need to see what their
positive function is; for unless we can assign them a positive function, we
shall find it difficult to explain why one divergence from "the prose line of
argument" is not as good as another. The truth is that the apparent irrelevancies which metrical pattern and metaphor introduce do become relevant
when we realize that they function in a good poem to modify, qualify and
develop the total attitude which we are to take in coming to terms with the
total situation.[49]

In addition to this disagreement with Ransom, Brooks does not
agree with Ransom's dualistic treatment of the cognitive and

[48] *Ibid.*, pp. 288–9.
[49] *The Well-Wrought Urn*, p. 208.

emotive powers in man. Brooks views the poem as an 'imitation' or as 'a simulacrum of reality' that verbalizes man's unified experience of reality, as when he says,

> It is not enough for the poet to analyze his experiences as the scientist does, breaking it up into parts, distinguishing part from part, classifying the various parts. His task is finally to unify experience. He must return to us the unity of the experience itself as man knows it in his own experience. The poem, if it be a true poem, is a simulacrum of reality—in this sense, at least, it is an "imitation"—by being an experience rather than any mere statement about experience, or any mere abstraction from experience.[50]

If one insists, as Ransom does, on the behavioristic rather than the associative poet, would he then have to conclude that the major poets of the English renaissance and the American renaissance are poor poets—Shakespeare, at least in his sonnets, and Whitman, in the entire body of his work? Perhaps most of us might agree with Brooks when he says that the poem's unity is in tone and attitude as enveloping the total body of the poem. Perhaps we might understand poetic unity to be in the poet's configuration of self as responding to the impress of existence.

For example, we might ask ourselves if the great, symphonic opening of "Out of the Cradle Endlessly Rocking" fits Ransom's description of a behavioristic poem. Is there the hard, discursive, single development of metaphor here? Or is there, rather, an emotion, a remembrance, a realization that is poured forth symphonically, with crescendo, yet intelligibly? Repetitively, the simple syntax creates a verbal vortex about one experience, but the syntax is not substantially either behavioristic or logical. Here, ironically, we have the poetry of one of the greatest and certainly the purest associative poets of all time. Whitman's very principle of poetic movement is rhapsodic association that blooms out of a central experience. We listen with our inner ear:

> Out of the cradle endlessly rocking,
> Out of the mocking-bird's throat, the musical shuttle,
> Out of the ninth-month midnight,
> Over the sterile sands and the fields beyond,
>   where the child leaving his bed
>   wondered alone, bareheaded, barefoot,

[50] *Ibid.*, p. 212.

Down from the showered halo,
Up from the mystic play of shadows twining and twisting
    as if they were alive,
Out from the patches of briars and blackberries,
From the memories of the bird that chanted to me,
From your memories sad brother, from the fitful risings
    and fallings I heard,
From under the yellow half-moon late-risen and swollen
    as if with tears,
From those beginning notes of yearning and love
    there in the mist,
From the thousand responses of my heart never to cease,
From the myriad thence aroused words,
From the word stronger and more delicious than any,
From such as now they start the scene revisiting,
As a flock, twittering, rising, or overhead passing,
Borne hither, ere all eludes me, hurriedly,
A man, yet by these tears a boy again,
Throwing myself on the sand, confronting the waves,
I, chanter of pains and joys, uniter of here and hereafter,
Taking all hints to use them, but swiftly leaping beyond them,
    a reminiscence sing.[51]

This is the beginning of the song of a poet, realizing his solitary destiny and vocation, a song which works itself associatively, repetitively, in aria-like movements, saturating the reader with the poet's realization of his vocation, his agony of non-fullfillment in the beloved and with his irrepressive love for mankind. If Whitman could not have worked horizontally or associatively instead of vertically or sequentially, we would not now have a Whitman. He works somewhat as Emerson does in his essays, approaching a realization from different stances, deepening the realization by his change of view. Whitman's poetry is like the ocean, moving magnificently, irregularly, with its debris or cataloguings, in its rhythms, in its crescendic swellings overwhelming the viewer and the listener on the strand of ordinary reality. We could abstract our 'prose discourse' or our 'logical core', but this would not be Whitman, nor what Whitman felt, and really would not be any part of Whitman's poem. Whitman has given his response to reality; he has configured his agony, and no logic will replace it.

Thus far in this chapter, we have seen what is the extrinsic formal cause of the poem for Ransom, namely, the poet's pure

[51] Walt Whitman, "Out of the Cradle Endlessly Rocking", *Complete Poetry and Selected Prose*, ed. James E. Miller, Jr. (Boston, 1959), p. 181.

universal, and what is the intrinsic formal cause, namely the concrete universal; we have seen that the object of the poem is no
longer, in 1955, just the 'beloved objects' of reality, but the poet's
realization and poetic structuring of the objects of reality. This
realization, poetically structured, would be Ransom's 'concrete
universal', the poetic marriage of matter and form. Finally, we have
seen that the metaphor is the most apt form of the concrete universal and, though it may be in tension with logic, it should be,
paradoxically, controlled and developed by it. In conclusion, let
us try to induce from Ransom's texts a general idea of the poem
that will, hopefully, approximate Ransom's fully matured idea.

D. AN INDUCTION TOWARDS RANSOM'S IDEA OF THE POEM

The central concern of Ransom in his early, important writing
on poetry (1934–38) was that poetry was the aesthetical, non-
devouring, non-scientific, and non-pragmatic recovery of the world,
generally within an established metrical form.[52] In the late thirties,
the objects of the world, which become the objects of the poem,
are realized as having a 'prose core' or 'logical core' and a 'tissue
of irrelevancy', and it is the tissue that keeps the object from being
scientific, and insures its being 'poetical or entire'.[53] The poem is
expressive, but it is expressive of the object, the 'world's body'.[54]
In *The New Criticism*, the duality of logic and irrelevance, and
structure and texture, is intensified[55] along with his insistence that
the poem is an ontological, not a scientific, structure.

About 1947, the poem becomes referential to the poet's state
of mind, and there are now 'id' and 'ego' levels in the poem that are
in tension with one another.[56]

[52] e.g. *The World's Body*, pp. 224–5; *The New Criticism*, p. 226; concerning
his early disposition to established metrical forms, see *The Fugitive* VI,
No. 3 (1922), 68. Here he implies that contemporary American poets have
too hastily given up established metrical form.

[53] *The World's Body*, p. 349.

[54] *Ibid.*, p. 254.

[55] Also in such essays as "Inorganic Muses", *Kenyon Review*, V (Spring,
1943), 278–300.

[56] "Poetry: The Formal Analysis", *Kenyon Review*, IX (Summer, 1947),
pp. 436–56, and "Poetry II: The Final Cause", *Kenyon Review*, IX (Autumn,
1947), 640–58.

In 1955, Ransom makes his last important critical change of view concerning the nature of the poem when he considers the poem as a concretization of a human universal of some nuance of existence.[57] Thus, taking the long, inductive view of Ransom's notion of the nature of the poem and including all those characteristics on which he has insisted, one might say that the poem is an unpragmatic attempt to embody metaphorically a universal of man's existence in the world, within a metered and logically structured tissue of words.

This consideration of the nature of the poem brings us naturally to the consideration of the parts or directions of the poem which will be, partly, the subject of the following chapter.

[57] "The Concrete Universal: Observations on the Understanding of Poetry", *Kenyon Review*, XVII (Summer, 1955), 383–407; reprinted in *Poems And Essays*.

IV

THE COMPOSITION OF THE POEM,
THE TYPES AND THE END OF POETRY,
AND THE QUALITIES OF THE POET

A. THE COMPOSITION OF THE POEM

In "Shakespeare at Sonnets", Ransom manifested his concern for intelligible form in the poem and for intelligible matter which is susceptible to criticism. The edifice of critical theory, for Ransom, cannot be built upon the shifting sands of emotion. In that essay, he hoped that the poet might control his metaphor to embody his universal. Ransom emphasized logic, there, because he opposed emotionalism and associative poetic progression. Yet Ransom is not characteristically single in his vision, and he is not generally an advocate of sheer logical development in the poem. He is split in his vision. He believes that as the particularity of the world always exceeds the ideas of the mind, so the texture of the poem will always overflow the logical core: he believes in 'heterogeneity-in-the-light-of-uniformity'.[1] Indeed, in one's study of Ransom, one must be patient with this oscillation of contextual emphases and, by his patience, one may know a criticism which is paradoxical but rarely over-simplified.

There is an evolution in Ransom's dual vision of the poem, and it is the understanding of this vision and its evolution that will be largely the subject of this chapter. In "Criticism, Inc." (1937), Ransom sees the poem as a tension of 'prose core' and 'tissue of irrelevancies'.[2] In "Yvor Winters: The Logical Critic" *(The New Criticism*, 1941), he sees the poem as a complex of meaning, having a logical structure and a texture, and a complex of sound, having meter and musical phrasing or texture.[3] In "Wanted: An Onto-

[1] "The Psychological Critic", *The New Criticism*, p. 92.

[2] *Virginia Quarterly Review*, XIII (Autumn, 1937), 586–602; also *The World's Body*, pp. 327–350.

[3] "The Logical Critic", *The New Criticism*, p. 211–275.

logical Criticism" of *The New Criticism*, he sees the poem as having its direct (intended) meaning and indirect (unintended) meaning and direct sound and indirect sound.[4] In this last essay, we notice Ransom employing tools that have a reference to the poet's mind. If he was before, he is not here the pure objective formalist. In 1943, in an essay entitled "The Inorganic Muses" he redefines his notions of 'prose core' and 'tissue of irrelevancies' as 'prose argument' and 'unstructured detail'.[5] Finally, in such essays as "Why Critics Don't Go Mad" (1952) and "The Concrete Universal: Observations on the Understanding of Poetry" (1955), he gravitates to the poetic division of metaphor, logic and meter.[6]

Ransom makes clear in "Criticism, Inc." that the object of criticism is the poem and the living tensions in the poem. He attempts, in that essay, to eliminate illusionary criticism: the illusions that the poem is not primarily an artefact, but a cause of psychological effect, or a simple idea, susceptible to paraphrase, or a means to biographical insight. He also wants to eliminate the illusion that the poem is a linguistic exercise in defining unusual words and identifying allusions, or that the poem is a moral study, seen in the light of a particular ethic.[7] The poem, for Ransom, "is an artistic object, with heroic human labor behind it, and on these terms calls for public discussion. The dialectical possibilities are limitless, and when we begin to realize them we are engaged in criticisms."[8]

Analytically, Ransom sees the poem as a 'universal' or a 'prose core' which tends to become the total aesthetic object, but which is impeded in this tendency by a web of words or 'tissue of irrelevancies'. The prose core is unable utterly to simplify itself in the reader's mind because it is held in a unique shape by the 'differentia', the 'residue' or 'tissue'[9] of the poem. To further explain this, one might say that red is impeded from becoming redness by a fabric and a man is impeded (in part) from becoming Man by the tissues in which he is incarnated.

[4] "An Ontological Critic", *The New Criticism*, pp. 279–336.

[5] *Kenyon Review*, V (Spring, 1943), 278–300.

[6] *Ibid.*, XIV (Spring, 1952), 331–339; also *Kenyon Review*, XVII (Summer, 1955), 383–407.

[7] *The World's Body*, pp. 343–45.

[8] *Ibid.*, p. 342.

[9] *Ibid.*, p. 349.

"The critic", Ransom says, "should find in the poem a total poetic or individual object which tends to be universalized, but is not permitted to suffer this fate. His identification of the poetic object is in terms of the universal or commonplace object to which it tends, and of the tissue, or totality or connotation, which holds it secure."[10] Yet, how will the critic know the universal? He will know it, says Ransom, in what may be centrally paraphrased: "it is a kind of story, character, thing, scene, or moral principle".[11] The tissue is what is irrelevant to our SIMPLE understanding of the subject or universal in the poem.

What the critic must confront, the poet must make. The style of the poet is distinguished by the general character of his irrelevancies or tissues. His poetic worth will be measured by the artistic deftness by which he impedes the emergence of the simple universal or prose object. The worth of the maker of stained glass windows, for example, is measured by the artistic impediment of white light by glass. The 'prose object', says Ransom, 'defines' the character of the POET, that is, his attitudes and his thoughts. The 'tissue of irrelevancies' manifests the character of the POEM, that is, its unique aesthetical perfection.[12]

Ransom realizes that this sort of analysis is a 'rude and patchy business in comparison with the living integrity of the poem',[13] but he sees it as the surest way to move to objective judgment and understanding of the poem. Indeed, one must pass from the simplicity of ignorance to some knowledge of analysis, and by analysis to the simplicity of authentic knowledge. Dissection, for Ransom, is not an end in itself but a means to know more fully 'the living integrity of the poem'.[14]

Ransom goes even more deeply and more precisely into poetic analysis in his essay "Yvor Winters: The Logical Critic" of *The New Criticism*. His fundamental thesis here is that the poem is an aesthetical being and should be apprehended as one. It should be examined and judged according to distinctions that are derived from the poem's nature. It should not be subject to the precepts of another area of human action, for example morality. The aesthe-

---

[10] *Ibid.*, p. 348.
[11] *Ibid.*
[12] *Ibid.*, p. 349.
[13] *Ibid.*
[14] *Ibid.*

tic, for Ransom, is beyond good and evil.[15] The Poem is not to be
used as a wheel for grinding one's moral axe. The Poem, for Ransom,
is not pure whatness or logical content, and the artist's mind
cannot and should not attempt to 'spiritually control'[16] this logical
content to attain a particular end. The total intention of the poet
is not something that begins the poem, but something that the poem
develops unpredictably. A poet does not determine to write about
some preoccupation and then do it, but he lets this preoccupation
be modified and, perhaps, transformed by the aesthetical demands
of the developing poem. The poem may drift laterally or obliquely
into another realization, because of the very exigencies of the verbal
material and the condition of time and space. Intention is known
only in terms of the finished poem, where the logical—perhaps
moral—content has acquired its irrelevance or its tissue that has
come to it through its aesthetical development. Ransom says:

> The total intention of the poem is something, but not an intention known
> to the poet at the moment when he begins to work up his logical content
> into a poem. Total intention is the total meaning of the finished poem, which
> differs from the original logical content by having acquired a detail which
> is immaterial to this content, being everywhere specific, or local, or parti-
> cular, and at any rate unpredictable. And what, precisely, is the poet's
> intention at the beginning? It is to write a poem, and that is, since he has
> written poems before, to turn his logical content loose to shift for itself in
> the world of fortuitous experience; to get out of the world of pure logical
> content. It is disrespect to the logic, if you are tremendously interested
> in the logic. If the given logical content is a moral one, it is a disrespect to
> morality in the degree that is a respect to something called poetic experience.
> Poetic experience is only to be had by disrespecting whatever kind of logical
> content we start with.[17]

Ransom is concerned in this essay with Winters' "frequent effort
to derive poetic structure ideologically".[18] He says that Winters is
"rash to declare that theological heresy unfits a poet for logical
poetry".[19] Indeed, Winters had criticized Jeffers for 'lack of moral
intelligence',[20] and in other essays had criticized Emerson, Poe and
Hawthorne as artists because they did not have an experience that

---

[15] "The Logical Critic", *The New Criticism*, p. 228.
[16] *Ibid.*
[17] *The New Criticism*, p. 224.
[18] *Ibid.*, p. 236.
[19] *Ibid.*, p. 227.
[20] *In Defense of Reason*, p. 34.

he considered sufficiently moral, or treat subject matter in a sufficiently human way.[21] Winters had declared artists unfit because they did not have the right ideas, or did not configure intelligibly what he termed plausible morality. For Ransom, this critical tendency is really uncritical because it is non-aesthetical. The poem is not a pragmatic or scientific structure that proves or persuades, but it is a structure that gives deft texture to a human experience.

Winters' response to Ransom in *In Defense of Reason* is that Ransom has contracted the meaning of 'moral' or 'ethical' to 'didactic'. What Winters means by moral is 'plausibly human'. Winters believes that when poetry becomes non-human, it thereby becomes unpoetic. Winters responds to Ransom in this fashion:

> The subject matter of poetry, on the other hand, is human experience; it can therefore be understood only in moral terms. The language of poetry is normal human speech, which was devised for dealing with normal human experience . . . when Ransom refers to my finding "that ethical interest is as frequent in poetry as any other one," he is again confusing the terms *ethical* and *didactic* and misunderstanding me in his own private fashion.[22]

After quoting a Ransom passage, Winters says, "This passage rests on the notion that moral content can only be didactic; that the content which is not didactic must be aesthetic. My own idea is that the term aesthetic has been used primarily to conceal a great deal of inaccurate thinking."[23]

It seems true that Ransom may have contracted Winters' notion of what is moral, but it is also true that he apprehends the restrictiveness in statements such as this: "I believe, to be sure, that ethical interest is the only poetic interest, for the reason that all poetry deals with one kind or another of human experience and is valuable in proportion to the justice with which he [the poet] evaluates that experience . . ."[24] But by what justice will the poet evaluate what human experience, Ransom asks in this essay. And does the poet really need to evaluate it? Maybe he is subject to it, confused by it or overcome by it. Does evaluation mean that the poet is implicitly getting off some moral dictum? Is this implicit

---

[21] In this treatment of these men in *In Defense of Reason*; pp. 262–282 and 577–603; 234–261; and 157–175, respectively.

[22] *Ibid.*, p. 506.

[23] *Ibid.*, p. 504.

[24] *Ibid.*, p. 505.

and, perhaps, subtle didacticism? In short, Ransom is more convinced than Winters that man is subject to existence and cannot always or in any place have his own intentional way. Not in life and not in art. Ransom is the critic of particularity, of unpredictability, of tentative and searching cognition. Winters is the critic possessed by the gleaming faith or gleaming assumption that man can and will determine himself, despite contingency in life and in art. Ransom says succinctly of Winters, "The remedy for unsatisfactory feeling—which I believe is the feeling of undecision—is, according to Winters, 'The waste-basket and a new beginning.' "[25]

Ransom, at any rate, is determined to criticize the poem as an aesthetical, not a moral structure, and therefore opens up the seventh part of his essay on Winters with a succinct notion of what he conceives the life of this structure to be.

> On the one hand, a poem is a complex of meaning, and it has two distinguishable features: a logical structure, and a texture. On the other hand, a poem is a complex of sound, and thus has its corresponding features: a meter, and a musical phrasing which is texture. Further, subordinating the sound to the meaning, in honor of the prejudices of our human interest, we have the meaning as a structure attended by sound as its texture; the relation obtaining both as a whole, and from moment to moment.[26]

We are able to see in this part of the essay what Ransom's attitude is towards free and metered poetry. There can hardly be a musical texture if there is no regular meter, for he believes that we can appreciate phonetic variation only against the background of phonetic regularity. The beauty of music lies in its luxuriance—a lapse, an extension, a syncopation—of the uniformity of sound. "This gives us", says Ransom, "a very good reason for wanting a meter; we are fond of phonetic texture of the phrases, and we cannot have it without the meter. The meter is the frame of reference against which we can locate and define phrases."[27] Here, as in other places, Ransom manifests his traditionalism, but a dynamic traditionalism. Meter makes for a more fertile phonetic texture, because the variations can be felt more dramatically against the background of a metered unity. Sound in poetry is structurally contrapuntal for Ransom. There is always the smooth regularity

[25] "The Logical Critic", *The New Criticism*, p. 228.
[26] *Ibid.*, p. 268.
[27] *Ibid.*, p. 269.

of structured melody countered by the startling, intuitive variations of emphatic or textured phrasing.

Winters, on this point of sound, agrees with Ransom that
metered poetry is a more effective phonic medium than freely
rhythmed poetry because it allows dramatic variation. But he
does not agree with Ransom in his notion of the unpredictable
texture or irrelevancy of sound. On this point, Ransom believes
that the roughening of meter is good in itself, as well as in the poem
as a whole, and that it results from the inability of regular meter
to synchronize itself with the logical structure of the poem.[28]
Ransom thinks that from this tension between logical structure
and meter there results a variation, a tissue, a texture of phonetic
irrelevancy. This unpredictability—this dynamic utterance of
sound—is an excellence for Ransom, even though it is irrelevant
or a poetically rebellious part of the poem.

Winters cannot conceive of any part of the poem—in this case
sound—being irrelevant. Sound, meaning and the entire poetic
complex must be ordered to the expression of a moral experience.
The parts of the poem, for Winters, must be dynamically relevant
to the poem and the meaning of the poem. The entire meaning-
sound complex of the poem should be ideally under the spiritual
control of the poet, and give expression to his moral judgment
and to feeling, which is part of moral judgment:

And the total phonetic value of metrical language has the power to
qualify the expression of feeling through language. Since the expression
of feeling is a part of the moral judgment as I have here defined it, the meter
has moral significance, for it renders possible a refinement in the adjustment
of feeling which would not otherwise be possible.[29]
. . . .
. . . In traditional verse, each variation, no matter how slight, is exactly
perceptible, and as a result can be given exact meaning as an act of moral
perception.[30]

In reply to Winters' insistence on the relevancy of meter in the
poem, Ransom has this to say: "It is not the business of the meters
to be expressive of meaning. Carry their expressiveness a little
further and the meters vanish in prose, and no felt phonetic quality remains to serve as an objective texture to meaning. Meter is

[28] *Ibid.*, pp. 259–61.
[29] *In Defense of Reason*, p. 551.
[30] *Ibid.*, p. 129.

like metaphor: the moment the metaphor is perfectly subdued
to its logical function in the meaning it ceases to be metaphor."[31]

In his treatment of structure and texture in relation to meaning
as distinguished from sound, Ransom gives an example of his own
so that we can see the 'logical structure' and the 'local texture'
at work in the poem—at least in part of the poem. His example
is Marvell's "To His Coy Mistress". He explains that the argument
is commonplace in this poem as it is in most poems. But without
the argument there can be no poems, for the texture 'depends'
on but is not determined by the 'logical structure'.[32] These two
elements are non-autonomous, but one is only loosely determined
by the other. Here again we see a core of difference between Ransom and Winters. Ransom says that the "logical core" of the poem
would be brought into poetic existence and would be more controlled by 'texture', than texture would be controlled by 'logical
core'. Winters maintains that it is the intense 'spiritual control'[33]
of the poet that fuses the complementary aspects of the poem, that
is, the denotative and connotative meanings of the poem. For
Winters, the poetic realization of the author would be spiritually
controlled to the extent that it would elicit proper 'connotations'.
For Ransom, the process would be more unpredictable; the textures—arising out of the difficulty and conditions of languages—
would give verbal dimension to the poet's realization or logical
core. For Ransom, the process of development in a poem, or the
process of creation in a poet, is a movement from simple realization
in the mind to a phrase that textures the realization and stimu-
lates the creative mind into spinning further texture and further
poetic suspension, until the original realization has been textured into the web of poetic existence. Ransom would also say that
the central meaning of the finished poem would not directly corres-
pond to the original realization of the creator. Rather, the original
realization would be the stimulus that generated the concentrated
attention of the mind and startled the mind into spinning its verbal web. Ransom implies a great deal of subconscious activity in
the creation of the poem; there is an unpredictable predictability
about what is happening. The demands of language and the excres-

[31] "The Logical Critic", *The New Criticism*, p. 259.
[32] *Ibid.*, p. 271.
[33] *In Defense of Reason*, p. 21.

cences of the subconscious seem to influence the focus of the conscious mind in the creative act.[34]

The result of all this is of course the poem—in the following instance, Marvell's "To His Coy Mistress". Ransom makes clear that it is the 'luxuriate' elements or textures that give this poem its worth;　these luxuriate or texture its poetic argument. He says:

> The poetic argument, in comparison, is not highly distinguished;　it is comfortably general, and it is weakly regulatory. It is the member details that have all the distinction;　they luxuriate, and display energy in unpredictable ways, going far beyond the prescription or paraphrase. Behind "To His Coy Mistress", for example, is an easy argument to the effect that a lover, after pointing out the swift passage of time, reasons with his mistress that they had better love at once. Shall we have, then, a bit of the conclusion of the argument, where he makes the application? It comes out this way, in part:

> > Now let us sport us while we may,
> > And now, like amorous birds of prey,
> > Rather at once our time devour
> > Than languish in his slow-chapt power.
> > Let us roll all our strength and all
> > Our sweetness up into one ball,
> > And tear our pleasures with rough strife
> > Th[o]rough the iron gates of life;

> Where the least that can be said is that we have got a good deal more than we had hoped for;　that this detail has assumed a good deal more of independent character than could possibly have been predicted.

> The independent character of the detail is the texture of the poem, and it "depends" from the logical argument in a sense, though not closely determined by it. The possibility of the above passage is contained in the condition that we have a dialectical lover making an argument with his coy mistress.[35]

Ransom closes his treatment of the aesthetical relation of the structure and texture in the poem by giving us a practical sense of this relation. He gives a poetic strategy, really, that good poets employ and the great critics apprehend: the more complex the structure, the simpler the texture should be and the richer the texture, the simpler the structure should be. The trick, he thinks, is to keep the intelligibility, while heightening the richness, and to keep the richness without losing the intelligibility. And yet he says that it is even more than that—the magic is in the poet's

[34] "The Logical Critic", *The New Criticism*, p. 273.

[35] *Ibid.*, pp. 270–71.

intuitive comprehension of the total structure-texture relation; he must sense the total dimension of the poem—that he is moving in the right direction, employing the right poetic tensions—though he has not achieved total dimension yet.

This notion of poetic strategy seems to be a partial answer to the critics who attack Ransom's principle of 'structure and texture', or 'logic and irrelevancies', for in this context the poet sees the poem as a becoming whole. Ransom says:

> To define the structure-texture procedure of poets is to define poetic strategy, the last and rarest gift that is given to poets. For undoubtedly, there are far more poets, persons with specific powers of poetic phrasing, than there are poetic strategists, or persons able to use this power in the composition of whole poems. . . .[36]

In the chapter following "The Logical Critic" of *The New Criticism*, Ransom takes up the theme of poetic dichotomies again, but with a psychological reference. In this chapter termed "An Ontological Critic", he wishes to look from the creator's mind, and to show artistic tensions as they organically and unpredictably work from the artist's mind. His terms, in this essay, are DS for determinate sound, IS for indeterminate sound, DM for determinate meaning and IM for indeterminate meaning. Ransom explains the relationship between these four poetic elements in this way: The writer may have a determinate meaning but this meaning is soon modified by the initial determinate sound, namely, the meter he proposes to write in. The mutual modification of DS and DM results in IM, and is indeterminate meaning and indeterminate sound. But one might ask, "How are we to escape total unintelligibility, if in the end the poetic product is indeterminate?" Ransom answers this, to his own satisfaction, by introducing another distinction. On the one hand, the modification of the originally contemplated sound pattern (DS) does not result in chaos; it will result in 'roughening' of the meter which, if effected in the proper way, may improve the poem. On the other hand, the modification of the originally contemplated meaning (DM) can result in confusion or inaccuracy. To avoid this, the poet will reject that indeterminacy of meaning that does not approximate his originally determined meaning. He will not allow the determinate meaning to drift into confusion or inaccuracy. Ransom says:

[36] *Ibid.*, p. 275.

... There are two kinds of indeterminacy in IM, and I wish to show how
the poet in metering an argument yields reluctantly to the first, as to an
indeterminacy that means only inaccuracy and confusion, and then gladly
to the second, as to an indeterminacy that opens to him a new world of discourse ... he [the poet] tries to shift the language within the range of a
rough verbal equivalence, and to alter DM no more than is substantially
necessary.[37]

The poet may substitute a close synonym for a given word, he
may change an active to a passive construction, change a parti-
cipial to a relative clause, an adjective into a substantive, a noun
into a verb in order that the meter may be aesthetically roughened,
but not destroyed. The genius of the poet, for Ransom, is how he
handles the unpredictable demands of meter against meaning,
meaning against meter. For the great poet, these mutual intrusions
will stimulate imagination into brilliant but apt digressions. Ransom's notion of the making of the poem seems somewhat similar
to the contrapuntal improvisation in Dixieland music or other
modern music which is not utterly determinate. There is, here,
a determinate melody and beat but this is roughened — and sometimes brilliantly — by the artist whose imagination can stand the
test of the spontaneous intrusion of a beat and a melody deviate
from his own.

Ransom gives an example of DM being modified into IM by DS,
in Marvell's "To His Coy Mistress". He first quotes part of the
poem and then gives his comment on the lines:

> Had we but world enough and time,
> This coyness, lady, were no crime.
> We would sit down, and think which way
> To walk, and pass our long love's day.
> Thou by the Indian Ganges' side
> Should'st rubies find: I by the tide
> Of Humber would complain. I would
> Love you ten years before the flood,
> And you should, if you please, refuse
> Till the conversion of the Jews.[38]

. . . .

Refuse brings out of the rhyming dictionary *Jews*, which it will tax the
poet's invention to supply with a context; but for our present purposes the
poet has too much invention, for it gives him the historical period from the

[37] "An Ontological Critic", *The New Criticism*, p. 303.
[38] *Ibid.*, pp. 311–12.

Flood to the conversion of the Jews, which is a useless way of saying ten thousand years, or some other length of time, and which seems disproportionate to the mere ten years of the same context, the only other period mentioned.[39]

But Marvell's "peccadilloes of logic", says Ransom, are "all overshadowed and we are absorbed"[40] by the brilliancy of poetic innovation. And this is a principle of poetic creation for Ransom: the 'importations'[41] that the imagination introduces into the body of the poem are proportionate to the indeterminacy that lurks beneath the surface of our human situations. We recover the density of experience in the exquisite indeterminacy of the poem. "When Marvell is persuaded by the rhyme-consideration to . . . furnish his abstract calendar with specifications about the Flood and the conversion of the Jews", says Ransom, "he does not make these additions reluctantly. On the contrary, he knows that the brilliance of the poetry depends on the shock, accompanied at once by realism or naturalness, of its powerful particularity."[42]

Let us pass now to another essay that takes up the tensions within the poem, but from still another angle. In his essay "The Inorganic Muses",[43] Ransom treats again the parts or directions of the poem, by returning to and redefining his notions of structure and texture:

If the poetic discourse turns about its prose argument, we might call the latter its structure; and then texture suggests itself for the name of the ubiquitous and unstructured detail. These are the terms I have found myself employing, and the best that have occurred to me. A texture is a private character in the materials which is visible over and above their structural uses.[44]

In this stand and in this essay he meets with opposition — or what he apprehends as opposition — from Robert Penn Warren in Warren's essay "Pure and Impure Poetry".[45] In both these essays,

---

[39] *Ibid.*, p. 313.
[40] *Ibid.*, p. 316.
[41] *Ibid.*, p. 314.
[42] *Ibid.*, p. 314.
[43] *Kenyon Review*, V (Spring, 1943), 278–300.
[44] *Ibid.*, p. 287.
[45] *Ibid.*, pp. 228–54.

Ransom and Warren have quoted the same passage from Frederick A. Pottle's book, *The Idiom of Poetry*. It reads as follows:

> . . . It occurs to me that the element of prose is innocent and even salutary when it appears as— take your choice of three metaphors— a background on which the images are projected, or a frame in which they are shown, or a thread on which they are strung. In short, when it serves a *structural* purpose. Prose in a poem seems offensive to me when . . . the prosaisms are sharp, obvious, individual and ranked coordinately with images.[46]

This passage mirrors, for Ransom, the 'ontological' duality that exists in the poem, the duality of the predictable and the unpredictable, of the core and the indeterminate interpolations of the core. The poem has design and freedom from design as the world has design and a density which overflows design. But Warren does not like this duality, as Winters and Brooks have not[47]—and, generally, for the same reason: because he believes that the poem is a UNITY of complexity, that the poem aesthetically resolves the disparate and ironic intrusions in an experience. Poetry is not simply or PURELY this or that experience, but it is an IMPURE UNITY, and should have no real texture of irrelevance. Warren conceives structure as being the whole of the poem. There are discordant or impure elements in a poem but the dynamic intensity of the poet's imagination reconciles these elements into an impure (non-simplified) artefact. He has this to say about Pottle's passage quoted above.

> At first glance this looks plausible, and the critic has used the sanctified word *structural*. But at second glance we may begin to wonder what the sanctified word means to the critic. It means something rather mechanical— background, frame, thread. The structure is a showcase, say a jeweler's showcase, in which the little jewels of poetry are exhibited, the images. The showcase should not be ornamental itself ("sharp, obvious, individual," Mr. Pottle says) for it would then distract us from the jewels; it should be chastely designed, and the jewels should repose on black velvet and not on flowered chintz.

And Warren comes to the sharp edge of his argument, explicitly against Pottle and implicitly against Ransom when he says: "But Mr. Pottle doesn't ask what the relations among the bright jewels should be. Apparently, not only does the showcase bear

---

[46] *Ibid.*, p. 245.
[47] In the parts of *The Well-Wrought Urn* and in *In Defense of Reason* that we have already seen.

no relation to the jewels, but the jewels bear no relations to each other."[48]

Warren is not wide of the mark, for Ransom says concerning the 'jewels' or 'texture' that "It [texture] is ubiquitous; and to put it simply, it consists in interpolated material which does not relate to the argument."[49]

Ransom uses the words 'richness', 'fulness' and 'concreteness'[50] to connote the validity of his demand for a texture, which is not one with structure. Ransom has a Kantian idea of a poem as he has of the world. For him, there is no one-to-one relation between the mind and the world and there cannot be a direct relation between the poet's intention and the artefact. The poem never exhausts the poet's universal, but always overflows it unpredictably. This point of 'relevance' and 'irrelevance', of 'structure' and 'texture' will always be a point of contention between Ransom and other critics. Some of them would say that Ransom is paradoxical, if not contradictory, when he insists that the poet make the right choice of irrelevance. These last four words are, at least, a semantical contradiction.[51]

Finally, in "Why Critics Don't Go Mad" (1952), Ransom arrives at the last stage of his analysis of the tensions of the poem. In this essay he explains that logic and metaphor and meter give a trinitarian existence to the poem. The 'logic' here would be the 'structure' of other Ransom essays, and the 'metaphor' here would be somewhat akin to the 'texture' of other essays, for it would overflow the 'logic' or 'structure'. Yet the metaphor in this essay also approximates the universal of the poet's mind and actually gives form to the logical structure. The metaphor, in the context of this essay, cannot be taken as an authentic 'tissue of irrelevancies' or 'texture'. It alters, gives dimension, expands and ramifies the logic, but is not irrelevant to it. Ransom implies a closer relation between logic and metaphor in this essay than between the poles of his older dichotomies when he says:

A little while ago I was urging Brooks to acknowledge the logical form of the poem as something fixed and—for the hard-headed English-speaking

[48] "Pure and Impure Poetry", p. 245.
[49] "The Inorganic Muses", p. 286.
[50] Ibid., p. 288.
[51] See In Defense of Reason, p. 540.

public—invincible; which the showy metaphors, episodic or dominant as they might be, had better make their peace with, especially since it would do them no harm; and I had the idea of the poem as a great paradox, a construct looking two ways, with logic trying to dominate the metaphors and metaphors trying to dominate the logic and neither or both (as we have in paradoxes), succeeding.[52]

So much for the logic and the metaphor. The 'meter', in this essay, would modify the meaning of the poem, as it did in previous essays. It would also startle the reader from his metronomic complacency, making him awake to the meaning of the phrase and to the counterpoint, by a phrase overriding the general sound structure. Donne, Ransom says, does not always 'jingle' but he 'jangles' and all good poets should to some degree "deserve hanging for not keeping accents". The meters should always be taskmasters for the writer and for the reader:[53] for the writer, as a proof of his authenticity—that he does not oversimplify; for the reader, so he will realize and awaken to what is going on in the poem. The 'felicity'[54] of metronome language is too bland a diet for Ransom, and he will soon leave a poem if it proceeds with mechanic regularity and predictability. "At first, the meters of a good poem, such as Donne and the metaphysicals usually write, seem to be restrictive and obstructive, upon the flow of language", says Ransom, "but actually they are what makes the phrases shine."[55] Part of the poem's beauty and life, for Ransom, is in its syncopation.

Ransom has not only concerned himself with the divisions such as logic, metaphor, and meter within the poem, but has also analyzed the genre of poetry and divided it into certain types. This was done most famously and perhaps most well in "Poetry: A Note in Ontology", which first appeared in *The American Review*[56] and was later printed in *The World's Body*. In understanding this division and these types, we will further understand what the matter of poetry should be for Ransom and how he thinks the metaphysical poets most artfully embody this matter.

[52] "Why Critics Don't Go Mad", *Poems and Essays*, p. 157.
[53] *Ibid.*, p. 156.
[54] *Ibid.*, p. 157.
[55] *Ibid.*
[56] *The American Review*, III (May, 1934), 172–200.

B. THE TYPES OF POETRY

1. *The Types of Poetry According to Subject Matter*

Ransom divides poetry into the physical, the Platonic, and the metaphysical. The basis of this division is his split of existence into things and ideas. For example, the recovery and imaging of physical things is the work of the physical poet, the tailoring of image to the propagation of idea is the work of the Platonic poet, but the dynamic and tenuous coordination of thing, idea and image is the achievement of the metaphysical poet. The metaphysical poet adjusts the idea to the unpredictable thing and to its verbal counterpart the image.

Physical poetry, for Ransom, is imagistic poetry, for it is only by images that you recover the thing. This poetry is a revolt against the nineteenth-century tendency to cap the world with an oversimplified moral and robe it with an opiate rhythm. "The imagists wished to escape systematic abstractness of thought, by immersing themselves in images."[57] " . . . The imagist's intention was to present things in their thingness, or *Dinge* in their *Dinglichkeit;* and to such an extent had the public lost its sense of *Dinglichkeit* that their redirection was wholesome."[58] But Ransom thinks that man could not and cannot, have a capacity for a 'disinterested interest'[59] in things as purely things, that is, things without any halo of idea about them. Thus, physical or imagistic poetry that outlasts the time in which it was created and that satisfies man will be 'impure' physical poetry, that is, poetry with a surreptitious ideational content. Ransom says that Amy Lowell n some lines from her "Thompson's Lunch Room, Grand Central Station", comes very close to 'pure' physical poetry, which for most of us is inconsequential:

> Jagged green white bowls of pressed glass
> Rearing snow-peaks of chipped sugar
> Above the lighthouse-shaped castors
> Of Gray pepper and gray-white salt.[60]

---

[57] "Poetry: A Note in Ontology", *The World's Body*, p. 117.
[58] *Ibid.*, p. 113.
[59] *Ibid.*
[60] *Ibid.*

But even here Ransom sees some evidence of mind in the meter that the mind has given to the poetry. There is some order of movement and some arrangement of objects in the poem. But this 'astonishing exhibit'[61] of nearly pure physical poetry evidences the reason, Ransom implies, that Miss Lowell's poetry will not endure—it is not sufficiently human. It is not an artful correlative for thinking man. Ransom abhors disembodied abstraction, but he also sees the need of thematic content.

Platonic poetry, which is the second category of Ransom's poetic division, tries its best to look like physical poetry "as if it proposed to conceal its medicine, which is the idea to be propagated, within the sugar candy of objectivity and *Dinglichkeit*".[62] As an example of this type of poetry he quotes the excerpt from "Pippa Passes" that has been cited in a previous chapter: "The year's at the Spring/And day's at the morn . . ." We are led to believe by this type of poetry, Ransom thinks, that man is capable of knowing and ordering existence by the power of his mind, that contingency does not constantly invade our privacy and sometimes destroy our intentions. Platonic poetry is, for Ransom, "transparent homilectics or allegory . . . translatable at every point into ideas".[63]

Both physical and Platonic poetry are deficient because they are unbalanced. The latter tries to promulgate ideas through images, the former is almost purely image with little idea. We are torn, as men, between the Platonism in us which is 'always sciencing and devouring',[64] and an instinct towards innocence—the love and the knowledge of objects in themselves. We are torn between the impulses to use the world, intentionally, both as an instrument for our own gratification and as an end in itself that might reveal to us its beauty and reality. We are torn between the principle of science which is abstraction and the principle of art which is perception. The poetic impulse is not free. It cannot gravitate to the pure perception of beloved objects; it is suspended above the pure ontology of objects by the practical, human instinct for ideas.[65] Is there, then, any poetic activity or type of poetry that

[61] *Ibid.*, p. 114.
[62] *Ibid.*, p. 121.
[63] *Ibid.*, p. 122.
[64] *Ibid.*, p. 130.
[65] This suspension of man above 'innocence' and immediate perception may indeed be Ransom's notion of the Fall of Man. It is implied in his work.

can satisfy man's suspended nature? Ransom says that there is, and he calls it metaphysical poetry. "Metaphysics, or miraculism, informs a poetry which is the most original and exciting and intellectually perhaps the most seasoned . . ."[66]

The specific literary means by which the metaphysical poet miraculously and yet humanly embodies his realization is the conceit. "Metaphysical poetry refers perhaps almost entirely to the so-called 'conceits' that constitute its staple. To define the conceit is to define small scale metaphysical poetry."[67] The conceit, for Ransom, is the developed metaphor. It originates and blooms out of metaphor. It is this seventeenth-century courage to boldly metaphorize that sets it apart from any other century, especially the nineteenth. The nineteenth century, Ransom thinks, was a century of simile — of circumlocution of the given experience, rather than the direct communication of the experience by metaphor. "One century was pithy and original in its utterance, the other prolix and predictable."[68] Ransom likes his poetry, it seems, the way Hulme did: hard, dry, succinct and startling — directly surprising. Although he recognizes the necessity of 'irrelevancy' in the poem, he does not like vagueness or the periphrastic construction where boldness is needed. And the metaphor is bolder, for Ransom, than the simile. It is a more direct commitment to things as they are and to experience as it is. If one says something is LIKE something else, it is less than saying it IS something else. Even at their boldest, Ransom thinks that the nineteenth century poets were generally inept in the use of metaphor. For example, he contrasts the direct and substantial metaphors of Donne's lines:

> Our hands were firmly cemented
> By a fast balm which thence did spring;
> Our eye-beams twisted, and did thread
> Our eyes upon a double string . . .[69]

with these lines from Tennyson, who Ransom thinks is only affecting a metaphor:

> Come into the garden, Maud
> For the black bat, night, is flown.

[66] "Poetry: A Note in Ontology", *The World's Body*, p. 135.
[67] *Ibid.*, p. 137.
[68] *Ibid.*
[69] *Ibid.*, p. 136.

"These lines", he says, "leave us unpersuaded of the bat."[70] The 'miracle'[71] of the metaphor, which is the core of the poem, must have its basis in verisimilitude. The likeness between the objects in the metaphor can only be partial but it must be substantial. Tennyson's bat, Ransom thinks, is only slightly and accidentally like the night, and it is a passing metaphor that is not developed and leaves us, really, unconvinced. Meter has been the tyrant here and metaphor has suffered.[72]

The 'miracle' in metaphysical poetry, for Ransom, is that it gives a 'local habitation and a name' to things which are really unutterable. It gives measure to the immeasureable and body to the ineffable, by speaking metaphorically. Here we come to an important facet of Ransom's understanding of poetry and of metaphor: metaphor in its historical dimensions is myth. Poetry is religion insofar as religion is myth, and insofar as it tries to make God ontologically realizable to the people in scripture, in ceremony and in prayer. Poetry gives to God in religion "a nature, a form, faculties, and a history; to the God, most comprehensive of all terms, which, if there were no poetic impulse to actualize and 'find' Him, would remain the driest and deadliest among Platonic ideas."[73] Authentic poetry, which Ransom here terms metaphysical poetry, is a substantial and committed way of making men realize the beloved objects of existence and the mythic source of that existence which man calls God.

2. The Types of Poetry According to End

In his essay "Poets Without Laurels" (1934),[74] Ransom divides poets and poetry more according to end than subject matter. The 'poets without laurels' are those who do not "identify with the public interests",[75] and therefore are not read by the general public. These poets do not care about the traditional and pragmatic

---

[70] Ibid., p. 138.

[71] Ibid., p. 135.

[72] Ibid., pp. 139–140.

[73] Ibid.

[74] Yale Review, XXIV (Autumn, 1934), 503–18, reprinted in The World's Body.

[75] "Poets Without Laurels", The World's Body, p. 56.

end of poetry—of making "virtue delicious".[76] They fear that by joining the moral with the aesthetic the aesthetic will suffer, with a resulting vitiation of the intrinsic worth of poetry. These poets without public laurels are the modern poets, not as Edna St. Vincent Millay and Robert Frost are modern but as Allen Tate and Wallace Stevens are modern. These two latter poets do not explicitly care about the strengthening of the public character; they have departed from the traditional compound of the moral and the aesthetic. Frost, Millay, Masefield, and E. A. Robinson are really traditional, for Ransom, because they poetically care about "morals or God or native land".[77] They urge or move the reader to aspire to do well and attain some valuable end. They have some consciousness and care about 'the public interest' and the reader's personal development.

Thus, the traditional poet feels an explicit responsibility for man's moral development. The modern poet, for Ransom, does not feel this responsibility—at least explicitly. From this initial distinction between the traditionalist and the modernist, Ransom moves to another distinction within the moderns. There are the 'pure' and the 'obscure' poets.[78] The poetry of the pure poet is that in which the aesthetic has been totally dissociated from the moral. It is that type of poetry in which the author is not concerned with truth but with the exquisite or effective execution of subject matter. It is, in Ransom's words "nothing but poetry; it is poetry for poetry's sake, and you cannot get a moral out of it . . . the new poetry cannot count on any customers except those specializing in strict aesthetic effects".[79] In this category he puts Wallace Stevens, and he tries to demonstrate why he does by briefly examining Stevens' poem "Sea Surface Full of Clouds". For Ransom, this poem has to do with "presenting surface effects beheld at breakfast time 'after the slopping of the sea by night grew still' ". This poem has "calculated complexity", for Ransom, "and its technical competence is so high that to study it, if you do that sort of thing, is to be happy".[80] But it has no interest in the 'res publica',

76 *Ibid.*, p. 57.
77 *Ibid.*, p. 58.
78 *Ibid.*
79 *Ibid.*, p. 59.
80 *Ibid.*

and its "subject matter is trifling".[81] I am not sure whether Ransom, here, has picked the right poet for his 'pure' poet — and he may not have picked a right poem. Wallace Stevens seems to be one of the most cerebral poets of our time and his subject matter is usually not trifling. He is concerned in such poems as "The Idea of Order at Key West", "Sunday Morning", "Bantams in Pine-Woods", "Anecdote of a Jar", "The Man on the Dump" and others with the tension between the flux of existence and the imaginative order given to it by the human mind. Ransom may have even missed the point in the poem he talks about, for here again existence is given order by the imagination of man. Ransom inadvertently sees this order when he says, "The first surface made one think of rosy chocolate and gilt umbrellas; the second of chophouse chocolate and sham umbrellas; the third of porcelain chocolate and frail umbrellas. . . ."[82] Although the subject as stated is trifling, the subject in relation to Stevens' pervading theme throughout his poems is not trifling: the mind and the concentration of man's imaginative powers are the only hope for giving order to existence. As Ransom says, "nothing could be more discriminating than these details which induct us respectively into the five fields of observation."[83] Existence has been given colorful order by man's imaginative response to it.

Be that as it may, Stevens is a 'pure' modern poet for Ransom, but Tate is not. Tate is an 'obscure' modern poet for him. Tate has an important subject — perhaps even a moral one — but he masks it by an obscure style. Tate will build up 'irrelevance' deliberately in order to escape a moralizing sententiousness. Ransom gives, as an example of Tate's 'obscure' style, two stanzas from the "Death of Little Boys". Here are the two stanzas.

> Then you will touch at the bedside, torn in two,
> Gold curls now deftly intricate with gray
> As the windowpane extends a fear to you
> From one peeled aster drenched with the wind all day
>
> Till all the guests, come in to look, turn down
> Their palms; and delirium assails the cliff
> of Norway where you ponder, and your little town
> Reels like a sailor drunk in his rotten skiff.

[81] *Ibid.*
[82] *Ibid.*
[83] *Ibid.*

Images like the 'cliff of Norway' and the 'windowpane' do not for Ransom, reveal their meaning; they thus help mask the precise meaning of the poet, so that it will not be too blatant to the reader's mind.

But where does Ransom stand in all this? What sort of poetry does he prefer, in regard to end and execution? Is it what he calls traditional, modern pure, or modern obscure poetry? Does he prefer the explicit compound of the aesthetic with the moral, the 'pure' aesthetic effect through deft execution, or the implicit or obscure compound of the moral with the aesthetic? He answers this question in this way: "Personally, I prefer the rich obscure poetry to the thin pure poetry."[84] Theoretically, he likes Tate better than Stevens, although twenty years later he will rate Stevens above Tate. "The Death of Little Boys", he says, is more exciting than "Sea Surfaces".[85] But he prefers the deft and substantial traditional poem to both the 'pure' and 'obscure' modern poem, because he finds beauty, goodness, and truth more deftly and naturally compounded in the poetry of Milton and Vergil[86] than in that of Stevens and Tate. He says of the 'pure' and 'obscure' modern poetry in relation to the traditional, " . . . It seems to me a pity that [modern poetry's] beauty should have to be cloistered and conventional, if it is pure, or teasing and evasive, if it is obscure. The union of beauty with goodness and truth has been common enough to be regarded as natural. It is the dissociation which is unnatural and painful."[87] Stevens' poetry is a poetry of 'dissociation' of the good, the true, and the beautiful. Tate's poetry of 'mixture'—an artificial but dynamic mixture of the good, the true and the beautiful. (Lemonade is Ransom's physical analogy for this artificial poetic mixture). The poetry of Vergil and Milton is poetry of natural 'compound', having a single effect of the compound of the true, the good and the beautiful. (Salt is his physical example, here, of this natural poetic compound.) It is this poetry of 'natural compound' which Ransom thinks is the most apt poetic correlative to existence and man's participation in it.[88]

---

[84] *Ibid.*, p. 61.
[85] *Ibid.*
[86] *Ibid.*, p. 74.
[87] *Ibid.*, p. 72.
[88] *Ibid.*, pp. 73–74.

It should be the poet's end to recover and poetically shape this natural compound of existence.

C. THE END OF POETRY

Ransom's notion of the end, or final cause, of poetry has been pretty much the same over the years. He has said that the recovery of the world as existing in its full particularity (or natural compound) is the end and the material object of the poem: to know the beloved object of existence through the primary means of metaphysical image given sonic movement by meter. The image is as close as we can get to 'Das Dinge an sich' and the poem is the most authentic form of that knowledge which is 'innocent' and 'disinterested': "Knowledge without desire".[89] Ransom does not think the end of the poem is simply moral, as he believes Winters does, because he believes the superimposition of moral values on the world will pervert the world. If there is a moral theme in the poem, it must make its peace with and work through the contingency of existence. Contingency and unpredictability in the world is analogous to the irrelevance and unpredictability in the poem. The poet may start off with a 'good intention' in creating a poem. But the 'id' level of consciousness in union with his worldly circumstance may get the better of him and of the poem too — as the id gets the better of the ego in Antony's refrain "But Brutus is an honorable man." The poem, for Ransom, will drift with the drift of existence. It will be faithful to the artist's encounter with existence which is always shifting, never static, never really susceptible to abstraction. The end of the poem for Ransom is not the catharsis of Aristotle[90] nor the psychic therapeutics of Richards, for these degrade art to the level of a technical instrument for doing good to man. Art must be as near to the world as it possibly can be, yet it must have form that will give aesthetic distance. It must recover the world it must make man know and love what exists. It will, then, in its EFFECT, make man more human. Ransom has this to say about the end of the poem and the poet:

The critic should regard the poem as nothing short of a desperate ontological or metaphysical maneuver. The poet himself, in the agony of compo-

---

[89] "Forms and Citizens", *The World's Body*, p. 45.
[90] "The Mimetic Principle", *The World's Body*, p. 211.

sition, has something like this sense of his labors. The poet perpetuates in his poem an order of existence which in actual life is constantly crumbling beneath his touch. His poem celebrates the object which is real, individual, and qualitatively infinite. He knows that his sciences will disintegrate it for their convenience into their respective abstracts. The poet wishes to defend his object's existence against its enemies, and the critic wishes to know what he is doing and how.[91]

Art is a labor of love, which is authentically moral when it shows things as they are and not as we would like them to be.[92]

D. THE QUALITIES OF THE POET AND RANSOM'S RATING OF MODERN POETS

According to what we have seen in this chapter and in the chapters previous to this, we can come to the following conclusions. The basic quality of the authentic poet for Ransom is (1) that he have no interest but love for the world as it is; (2) that he be not too demanding about the absolute fitting of the world to the metaphors by which he will recreate it and recover it; (3) but that he will be demanding enough and deft enough to choose the right 'irrelevancies' so that the poem will not drift too far associatively, and thereby become unintelligible or splintered; (4) that the poet be very intimate with 'low grade music' of meters in order that "he may wake up the free imagination" and that "the poetic language . . . will respond instantly and surely to his occasion"[93]; (5) that the poet be such a master of image and meter—so imaginatively inventive—that he may work the 'logic' against the 'texture' and the meter against both, and still come out with something livingly exquisite; (6) that he be alive in mind as well as in emotion so that his poetry will not be tyrannized by the rhythmic effects of emotion, namely meter; and finally, (7) that the poet—although he works with a sort of 'unpredictability' and through 'irrelevance'—have an intuitive sense of poetic strategy, the "last and rarest gift that is given the poets."[94] This strategy is the power to see the phrase in the context of the whole poem that is coming into being: a

[91] "Criticism Inc.", *The World's Body*, p. 348.
[92] "The Mimetic Principle", p. 208.
[93] *Kenyon Review*, XIII (Summer, 1951), 447.
[94] "The Logical Critic", *The New Criticism*, p. 275.

sort of poetic clairvoyance to adjust what nearly is (the phrase) to what shall be (the poem).

In "Poetry of 1900–1950"[95] Ransom rates his modern poets. This rating is interesting because it gives explicitly those who Ransom thinks are the best minor poets, the best major poets, and a group of poets who are suspended between the categories of minor and major. He also outlines the qualities of modern poetry and the prominent characteristics of the major poet of the twentieth century.

The qualities of modern poetry, in the context of this discussion, are three for Ransom. The first quality as related to the second, is "an unusual mastery of strong imaginative idiom, marked no less by its abhorrence of fixed meters than by the imaginative quality itself."[96] Ransom implicitly lauds mastery of the imaginative idiom and perhaps would give William Butler Yeats as an example of this first quality, for he rates Yeats as one of the five major poets of the twentieth century. As a 'perfect example' of the second quality, he offers the "accomplished poet", T. S. Eliot, "who is sensitive to climactic environment and metaphysically wistful" and "is pretty sure to indicate here and there in the verse his entire command of metrical language, and to fall continuously and lovingly into metrical phrases; but he will draw the line against a working, responsible, overall metrical form."[97]

The third quality of modern poetry is "the quantity of hateful poetry; satirical poetry, having for its target the common behaviors of the age . . . It is the work of poets having the religious imagination and railing or grieving about its removal from the common context of life."[98] This sort of poet might also be exemplified by Eliot, whom Ransom mentions later in relation to hateful poetry. Eliot's "Hollow Men" or "The Waste Land" would seem to be what he means by 'hateful poetry'. There are both hate and grief in poems caused by man's loss of his spiritual heritage. The water of spirit has gone out of man and he has become a withered paralytic. This 'hateful poetry' also issues, he thinks, from a material savagery which is a part of the toughness of the modern age.

---

[95] Kenyon Review, XIII (Summer, 1951), 445–454.
[96] Ibid., p. 448.
[97] Ibid.
[98] Ibid., p. 449.

The poets who write this way "have been bred to the 'facts of life' more than to gentleness and Platonic ideas". They are concerned with the 'roughneck vigor of living'[99] and 'the animal grace which often goes with it'.[100] Ransom is not sure how he should judge the worth and the ultimate significance of this type of 'hateful' poetry, but he knows that the previous century was too 'soft' to hold these men and the characters they create. The Sweeney of the bath and the nightingales is an 'engaging barbarian' and Ransom is not sure that he is 'damned'.[101] "The Ballad of Billie Potts", by Robert Penn Warren, is a poem of the savagery of the 'new' man, and Ransom admires Warren's 'negative capability' in creating it.[102] Warren himself, says Ransom, is not savage, but he has the capability of realizing what savagery is, and the conditions and reasons for its existence.

His fourth and last generalization about modern poetry is its extreme 'condensation' and 'syntactical displacement'.[103] He does not give an example of a poet who writes or wrote this way, but anyone who has studied modern poetry can apprehend this trend issuing from poets such as Robert Browning, Emily Dickinson, Gerard Manley Hopkins, up through poets such as Eliot, Hart Crane and E. E. Cummings. The elision, the fragmented sentence, the half-utterance, the ellipsis, the inverted word order and a mosaic of images rather than an even poetic progression are some of the characteristics of this group of poets. Ransom also sees in this group that uses 'brilliant metaphors and glancing allusions' an obsessive reference to 'objects which are symbolic with religious meanings'.[104] This, for him, is further evidence of the frustrated and aspiring 'religious imagination'.

After outlining what he thinks are the characteristics of the modern age of poetry he offers 'a judgment so presumptuous' that he "must insist it is tentative", and 'anything but dogmatic'.[105] This judgment concerns the relative worth of modern poets from 1900 to 1950 who "have established themselves and have a good

---

[99] *Ibid.*, p. 450.
[100] *Ibid.*
[101] *Ibid.*
[102] *Ibid.*
[103] *Ibid.*, p. 450.
[104] *Ibid.*, p. 451.
[105] *Ibid.*

prospect of surviving a few half centuries".[106] He lists his group
of minor poets first, in order of their 'seniority', or age. The minor
poets are: Robert Bridges, Walter de la Mare, John Masefield,
Vachel Lindsay, William Carlos Williams, Ezra Pound, Marianne
Moore, E. E. Cummings, Hart Crane and Allen Tate.[107]

The next group he offers puts him in "an embarrassing predica-
ment". He is not sure whether these poets belong in his minor or
major categories, so he will put them in neither. To judge a poet
as major, Ransom uses "the criteria which will occur to everybody".
These criteria are, first, "that his deliveries should be of vital
human importance"; secondly, "that these deliveries be produced
rather consistently in some volume", and lastly, that they be produced "freshly rather than repetitiously". The four in-between
poets he names "have failed to have sufficient range of interest",
though they have "assured brilliances"; they also may have "veered
from one kind of poetry to another without making their second
poetry decisive".[108] These suspended poets are: A. E. Housman,
Wallace Stevens, W. H. Auden, and Dylan Thomas.

The following set of poets fulfill both the qualities of the major
poet in this essay and the qualities of the poet that I have drawn
from Ransom's writing and have outlined in this chapter. These
are Thomas Hardy, William Butler Yeats, Edwin Arlington
Robinson, Robert Frost, and T. S. Eliot.[109]

From these he chooses one "whom none of them will outweigh
or outlast".[110] This is Thomas Hardy. Ransom believes that
Hardy's theme is 'perennial', that there "always will be young
people who will have to make their painful adaptation to the brute
universe."[111] Hardy has saturated in his person the deep, tragic
vision of the hopeless and mortal struggle of mankind against
overwhelming and determined odds. Hardy also writes his poetry,
moreover, 'according to the book',[112] that is, he has a strong metrical
sense and he roughens his metrical forms brilliantly. Ransom is

---

[106] *Ibid.*

[107] *Ibid.*, p. 452.

[108] *Ibid.*, p. 452; all of the quoted phrases in this paragraph come from
p. 452.

[109] *Ibid.*, p. 453.

[110] *Ibid.*

[111] *Ibid.*

[112] *Ibid.*, p. 454.

very partial to the poet who moves his themes within established sound patterns, but still makes these patterns his own by giving them his own sonic texture of irrelevancy. Hardy has "at the bottom of his sixty-year-old mind [such a] deposit of sensitive experience that the metrical beauty has no trouble finding words".[113] Hardy also has the knack of giving every line he has written a life of its own by the deft placement of the 'quaint' or 'homey' word. His language does not have a 'second-handed rhetorical flavor'. In the eight-hundred pages of Hardy's poetry Ransom rarely finds an "unrewarding page or poem".[114] This is Ransom's pote and he has given his reasons why he is. Since Hardy is Ransom's choice as the major poet of the twentieth century, he may well have many of those qualities that Ransom thinks the poet should have: love of the objects of the world, a tentative and not dogmatic sense of order, a deft sense of choice in choosing the appropriate, textual irrelevancy, an intimate sense of 'low grade music' of meter, a strength of intellect to govern emotion, a concentration to develop the poetic metaphor and finally the "last and rarest gift that is given to the poet", the intuition to see the poem, implicitly, as a becoming whole.

---

[113] *Ibid.*
[114] *Ibid.*

V

CRITICISM AND THE CRITIC

Before going into what criticism and the critic are for Ransom, perhaps we should say what they are not. This method of analysis may more sharply delineate Ransom's notion of these two subjects.

Criticism is primarily and centrally not psychologism and not moralism, and the intent of the critic is neither to analyze a verbal artefact that is a correlative of a subjective state of mind, nor is it to explain this artefact in terms of its morality. Criticism is not psychologism, for Ransom, primarily because the poem is not reducible to subjectivity. The poem is concerned with man realizing the world and himself in the world. It is concerned with ontology or the knowledge of being in its most authentic sense, that is, in its living particularity and unpredictability. In short, the poem's subject matter is truth, not arbitrary and subjective illusion. The psychic harmony of man's impulses, in Ransom's opinion, is not sufficient reason or matter for a poem.

> The psychologistic critic holds that poetry is addressed primarily to the feelings and the motor impulses ... Mr. Richards came out spectacularly for the doctrine, and furnished it detail of the greatest ingenuity. He very nearly severed the dependence of the poetic effect upon any standard of objective knowledge or belief. But the feelings and impulses which he represented as gratified by the poem were too tiny and numerous to be named. He never identified them; they seemed not so much psychological as infra-psychological. His poetic was esoteric ... eventually his readers, and Richards himself, lost interest in it as being an improvisation much too unrelated to the public sense of a poetic experience.[1]

As poetry is not psychologism,[2] for Ransom, so it is not moralism. It is not moralism, because knowledge of being and love of the objects of the world, which are the subject matter and end of poetry,

---

[1] "Criticism As Pure Speculation", *The Intent of the Critic*, p. 95.
[2] *Ibid.*, p. 94.

are not pragmatic. Knowledge is an end in itself, and poetry is a fine art. It should not be used to grind one's 'moral axe'.[3] "Art is more cool [implying aesthetic distance and form] than hot, and a moral fervor is as disastrous to it as a burst of passion",[4] which implies the sheer pouring out of the personality without aesthetic distance. The poem is an aesthetic object, and the "business of the critic is exclusively with aesthetic criticism".[5] Though Ransom tempers his dislike of moral pragmatism as he grows older, as in "The Concrete Universal: Observations On The Understanding Of Poetry" (1955), he will always be centrally concerned with the poem as textured knowledge and not as propaganda or metered persuasion. He does not like his moral or human universal untextured.

Both psychologism and moralism are joined in Ransom's mind with scientism: that devouring, pragmatic instinct of man's mind together with the procrustean urge to put things and men in their place. Poetry's faithfulness to things as they are, without any want to crush them or tear them from what they are, distinguishes poetry from science.[6] Both have structure. Science has pure structure, but poetry has a structure with an unpredictable texture; the texture makes it faithful to the world, the structure makes it intelligible to the reader.

It is this structure-texture relation which should be the object of the critic's energy. It is William Empson's intense and close-reading sensitivity to this relation that makes Ransom call him an 'unequalled genius' in The New Criticism.[7] Empson has the ability to wring out every drop of ambiguity contained in the texture of the poem. He is able to illuminate the dimensions of poetic texture and uncover the layers of tissue in the poem. He has the subtle and refined mind that is able to discover living fullness in the design of the poem. Ransom has this to say about his subtle peer.

It does not seem impossible that we should obtain close studies of the structure-texture relations that the poets have actually found serviceable in the past. The best endowed critic in the world for this purpose might

[3] Ibid., p. 99.
[4] Ibid., p. 104.
[5] Ibid., p. 109.
[6] "Criticism, Inc.", The World's Body, p . 347.
[7] "Yvor Winters: The Logical Critic", The New Criticism, p. 275.

very well be, I should think, Mr. William Empson, the student of ambiguity. His studies up to date have been very valuable diversions, a little to the side of great critical problems. But he probably has an unequalled genius for evaluating the intangible sort of thing we call the poetic "situation". We have other valuable critics too, but their studies are not of anything so capital as this. To define the structure-texture procedure is to define poetic strategy, the last and rarest gift that is given to poets.[8]

Another critic who possesses the power to read closely and unravel the intertwined yet intelligible tissue of a given poem is Cleanth Brooks. Brooks is the critical publicizer and expositor of modern poetry. He has been making the world know and understand the modern poetry which is worthwhile. He is also, for Ransom, one of those who believe that modern poetry is, in part, a resurrection of the metaphysical poetry of the seventeenth century. Ransom, however, has reservations about this point. He believes that the moderns have neither the mastery of meter nor the consistency of logical argument in their poems which the metaphysical poets had in theirs. Ransom's central contention with his younger critic is that Brooks finds poetic unity in dramatized attitude. But psychological connotations of attitude or intention or tone do not promise sufficient poetic unity for Ransom; he wants a logical core to work from. Nevertheless, he has this to say about Brooks.

He is, very likely, the most expert living "reader" or interpreter of difficult verse. A very great service performed by his book [*Modern Poetry and the Tradition*] consists in the plain exposition of passages, and attribution to the authors of what, we will nearly always have to concede, must have been their "intention". The intellectual poets of our time have had no champion his equal.[9]

The primary object of criticism is the poem and the structure-texture relation within the poem. Thus, the first prerequisite of the critic is that he be a close reader who is alive to the many possible ways a word or a phrase can shine. The connotations of one word may oscillate in the mind indefinitely. The great critic—the close-reading critic in this case—must be able to distinguish as many oscillations as possible. He must be sensitive to the retardation or the acceleration of the movement of the line, the assonantal

[8] *Ibid.*

[9] "Apologia For Modernism", review of *Modern Poetry and the Tradition*, *Kenyon Review*, II (Spring, 1940), 248.

and consonantal quality of the line, the nuance of difference between any given word with another. In short, the intense and alive
scrutinization of the text—the full and fundamental understanding
of the poem—is still the critics's 'single role' for Ransom,[10] and
this ability to scrutinize the text is the critic's central prerequisite.

Within this category of close-reading critics, Ransom also includes Eliot and, to a lesser degree, Richards. Eliot's strength, for
Ransom, lies partially in his weakness: his ability to read a poem
intensively and accurately is derived from his strong power to
instantly compare texts.[11] He is the learned critic for Ransom;
he is aware of the breadth and depth of literary tradition, and
brings this awareness to bear upon the text. Eliot's sensitive
ability to compare and contrast texts makes him a great practical
critic, and gives him a foundation which is extremely important
to Ransom. Ransom lauds the critic who is what T. S. Eliot is:
a scholar.

Brooks will take his critical method and put it to work in a fury and spate
of words; I in my degree have been ready with a gabble of my own. But at
my shoulder I have sometimes seemed to sense a strong silent presence
attending and watching me. It is not Vergil, for he attends the poets; this
Guide for critics, as I sense his presence, is the Great Scholar, so modest
that he is anonymous, and in my vision I have never been able to identify
him; but perfect in his attainments; possessing the sense of art as wholly
as he possesses the text, in beautiful proportion and justice, yet intuitively,
without an effort; it is precisely because he has been a faithful scholar that
this grace has been added unto him. He causes me to be apprehensive that
my kind of criticism may be so partial as to belittle the poem, for he will
know at once, and it will be painful to see him register his embarrassment.[12]

Learning and scholarship, Ransom thinks, are another prerequisite for the great critic. They help to insure a full and close
reading of the text. Although Ransom disagrees with Eliot's impersonal theory of poetry in which the poet "operates in the capacity of a private secretary to the tradition",[13] and although Eliot

[10] "The Concrete Universal", *Poems and Essays*, p. 160.
[11] Eliot's strength, for Ransom, is in the horizontal plane of comparative
literature; not in the vertical plane of philosophic foundation and conclusion. On this point see Ransom's review of Eliot's *The Use of Poetry*,
Saturday Review of Literature, X (March 24, 1934), 574. See also footnote
no. 14.
[12] "Why Critics Don't Go Mad", *Poems and Essays*, p. 151.
[13] "The Historical Critic", *The New Criticism*, p. 147.

has "no great philosophical habit, nor philosophical will, to push through it [his critical sense] to a definition",[14] Ransom believes that there is in his writings "an immediate critical sense which is expert and infallible".[15] He is for Ransom—at least in 1934—"the most particularistic critic that English poetry and English criticism have met with. He does not like to raise his head from the text. And it is the source of his strength; nobody else is so constant in his reference to the thing in itself."[16] It seems to me that Empson, first, and then Brooks, may be more sensitive to poetic nuance than Eliot, but there is for Ransom no critic who exceeds Eliot in learning and in bringing the force that learning bears to the poem.

As for Richards, Ransom thinks that he is very sensitive to the affective nuances of a word, but that his criticism is vitiated by his subjectivism, which is a shifting base for criticism. Still within the category of close readers, Ransom thinks that Yvor Winters is the "enemy of confusion . . . and irresponsibility of craftsman",[17] but that his criticism is vitiated because he narrows and distorts the world by telling the poet what he must and must not write about. Winters is a sharp but narrow critic. In short, Ransom says that the 'psychologistic affective vocabulary' of Richards and the moralism of Winters are 'the two specific errors' that damage the new criticism.[18]

All of these men, in descending order, attend to the text and are close readers. Eliot is the scholar amongst them, and this may, indeed, raise him, for Ransom, above the 'unequalled genius' of Empson.

We have seen two prerequisites of the authentic critic for Ransom, and we have seen the critics whom he has considered as examples of these prerequisites. There is a third prerequisite, and this gives the critic his ultimate foundation. The prerequisite is a philosophy, and Ransom's examples are Kenneth Burke and R. P. Blackmur. We could also include Yvor Winters, but he suffers, in Ransom's optic examination, from myopia or, more exactly, from glaucoma, for his lateral vision—his width of vision—is

[14] *Ibid.*, p. 145.

[15] *Ibid.*

[16] Review of *The Use of Poetry*, *Saturday Review of Literature*, X (March 24, 1934), 574.

[17] "Yvor Winters: The Logical Critic". *The New Criticism*, p. 254.

[18] *The New Criticism*, p. xi.

limited. Winters is philosophic, but he is too narrowly and rigidly so. His acuteness is too cold and abstract, and is not fully open to the unpredictable yet exquisite fullness of the world and the poem.

Ransom wants an ultimate and rooted understanding of poetry and poems. He wants the critic to know radically why a thing is so, and not otherwise. The critic must have a passion for Being—for the recovery and the understanding of things as they are. Ransom gives due and full credit to the psychological critic, Richards, the historical critic, Eliot, and the logical critic, Winters, but he calls out in the last chapter of *The New Criticism:* "Wanted, an ontological critic", a critic with an open and yet a radical knowledge of Being. He says in "The Concrete Universal: Observations On The Understanding of Poetry",

> I don't know how it is possible to deny to the literary critic the advantages of philosophy; I suppose we have fears that he, or his audience, will be unequal to them. But does he not try for a radical and a decisive understanding of poetry? . . . The reading of technical philosophy is the critic's homework. It should be fruitful of radical and decisive ideas— if his mind is strong enough to take them.[19]

In the opening passage of "The Cathartic Principle", he sardonically reinforces this notion, when he writes: "The good critic cannot stop with studying poetry, he must also study poetics. If he thinks he must puritanically abstain from all indulgence in the theory, the good critic may have to be a good little critic."[20]

Yet Ransom does not wish us to misunderstand him. There are two qualities, or really two facets of one quality that will save the authentic critic from being a cold, professional philosopher. He must, first of all, be faithful to things as they are, to what Coleridge, in his essay "On Poesy Or Art", calls 'natura naturans', as distinguished from 'natura naturata'. Things and the world and the poem are not static to Ransom, and knowledge of these is not static either. Ransom's critic must be an *a posteriori*, inductive critic; not an *a priori*, absolutist critic. The critic must gather his knowledge from changing reality and from changing philosophy, which is the radical knowledge of reality. In respect to this point Ransom says:

[19] "The Concrete Universal", *Poems and Essays*, pp. 159–60.
[20] "The Cathartic Principle", *The World's Body*, p. 173.

The critic can hardly run the risk of deferring to the professional philosopher. A professional philosophy tends to rise crazily upon its base, and
after it has got a certain distance from the ground to collapse like Babel in
a confusion of jargon. It has happened again and again in the history of
thought. A school tumbles, and then thinking can begin all over again; and
philosophy is cyclic in action, like business, and like civilization. It has to be
renewed every generation or so; and it is not likely anyway that one generation can live on another's philosophy.[21]

The critic must keep his resiliency, his warmth and his intimacy
with the text. This is the second facet of the one quality referred
to above—intimacy. The critic must be INDUCTIVE and he must
be INTIMATE with human experience and with poems which are
of human experience in order to escape the coldness of the professional philosopher. If Ransom thought that philosophy would
cause rigidity in the critic, he would forego philosophy. But he does
not think this to be a necessary effect of philosophy.

I could believe that he [the critic] should be denied if I thought it must
follow that having once got into philosophy, he would never get out again.
This would mean that resiliency had gone for some reason from his working
consciousness, that the fateful time had come when the usual succession
of its moods and interests must break down; which would be distressing
if it did not seem arbitrary.[22]

The critic has one great advantage over the philosopher in the
examination of a poem: "he is intimate, and it must be very rare
if they [the philosophers] are intimate, with the immediate pulsing
fact of the poem".[23]

It is on these points of philosophy and intimacy that Ransom
both lauds and criticizes Kenneth Burke. Ransom says, "Of all
our critics Burke is philosophically the subtlest, temperamentally
the most ironical. The irony precludes a notable human warmth
and the cool tone repeals weak readers as much as the speed and
range of his dialectical shifts."[24] Nevertheless Ransom acknow-
ledges Burke's "sophistication and commitment".[25] Ransom sees
Burke as a 'modern humanist', interested in human experience,
but trying to over-categorize human experience and its resulting

[21] *The World's Body*, p. 177.
[22] *Poems and Essays*, p. 159.
[23] *Ibid.*, p. 160.
[24] "Mr. Burke's Dialectic", review of *A Grammar of Motives*, *New Republic*,
CXIV (February 18, 1946), 257.
[25] *Ibid.*

language with the stiff forms of *a priori* thought. Ransom thinks
him agile in dialectic, but not completely and flexibly faithful to
the fullness and unpredictability of existence, human experience,
and the various genres of verbal art. Burke's rigid pentad of act,
scene, agent, agency and purpose, the categories of his *A Grammar
of Motives*, cannot be the categorical suits to which all verbal art
will be fit. Burke's categories are dramatic and, as such, are limited
in the scope of their application. Burke's "humanistic [here, im-
plying rational motive] bias", says Ransom, "enters into his choice
of categories. Burke's grammar is dramatistic. Drama occurs for
him when the turn of events is, as in the play, with purposive
acts which are more than 'motions' of science, and moral agents
which are more than 'bodies'."[26]

Ransom considers Burke Hegelian in his dialectical agility, but
Platonic in his formalism.[27] It seems that, for Ransom, Burke has
not fully retrieved himself from philosophy. Concluding his review,
he has this to say of Burke's dramatic categories in *A Grammar of
Motives*.

> At any rate it seems to be the testimony of history that many events
> are not suited to drama, for they have gone into fiction. Still other events
> must not be suited to fiction, for they have gone into poetry. All the time and
> everywhere, there is a multitude of events not much suited to any of these
> arts because they are peculiarly suited to science. And if science does well
> in not aspiring to poetry, it does well also in not aspiring to drama. Perhaps
> the same thing may be said of philosophy.

As we saw in the first chapter, Burke is too Platonic or formalistic
for Ransom, but he is subtle enough to be important to him. Burke
has partly mistaken the logical for the ontological. He has done,
to some extent, with dramatic categories what Winters has done
with moral categories: suited reality to them, though the suit
may be a bad fit.

So Burke is subtle but deficient. Whom then do we find as a
critic with philosophical depth and width, and with the power
to handle deep insights resiliently and without the jargon of the
philosopher? Jargon, for Ransom, is symptomatic of philosophical
abstraction—of critical separation from the warmth of the text.
"Probably the critic's ordinary job is to interpret the poem",

---

[26] *Ibid.*
[27] *Ibid.*, 257–8.

he says, "in common language that is not philosophical and does not stray far from the literary text . . .".[28] Is there a critic who has visional depth and width and the resilient warmth that Ransom wants? No critic fills this description completely, but I think that R. P. Blackmur comes closest to it. Blackmur is open, eclectic, knowledgeable and very close-reading. He is attentive to the visions of the philosophers and the interweavings of the text. He will ignore no trend in philosophy or criticism, but will hold none completely. And he will use every means available to illuminate the structure-texture relation within the poem. In fact, the following quotations sound very much like Ransom, but it is Blackmur who is speaking.

> All fall notwithstanding, for as knowledge itself is a fall from undifferentiated sensation, so equally every formula of knowledge must fall the moment too much weight is laid upon it — the moment it becomes omnivorous and pretends to be omnipotent.[29]
> . . . .
> Poetry is life at the remove of form and meaning; not life lived, but life framed and identified. So the criticism of poetry is bound to be occupied at once with the terms and the modes by which the remove was made and with the relation between . . . content and form.[30]

Blackmur's terms are not the same as Ransom's, but his attitude towards life, poetry, and art are similar. He believes the philosophy and doctrine are not ends in themselves, but means to understanding man's experience and the verbal form of man's experience in art.[31] Ransom has this to say of Blackmur in his preface to *The New Criticism.*

> Mr. R. P. Blackmur is a distinguished critic, and no other living critic is less apt to take unassimilated the formulas of the profession and apply them hastily to the poem. His critical writing gives us the sense of materials turned over a great many times, and carried into the light of the usual illuminations. (I do not mean that they are not exposed also to some illuminations made at home.) The writing is close, and a little difficult, rather than simple and systematic as it might be if a critic had been shallower and more obliging . . . He is distinct, and repels the tag of common category,

---

[28] "The Concrete Universal", *Poems and Essays*, p. 159.
[29] "A Critic's Job of Work", *The Double Agent, Essays in Craft and Elucidation* (New York, 1935), p. 270.
[30] *Ibid.*, p. 269.
[31] *Ibid.*, p. 271.

he is nevertheless a "new" critic in the sense of this book . . . he has mastered some or all of the critical systems in this book . . .[32]

Blackmur is concerned with the structure-texture relationship of the poem, and is close-reading the way Empson is; he is a scholar, but possibly not to the extent that Eliot is, and he is more open to evolution in philosophy and art more than is Burke. He does not, however, escape Ransom's criticism in "The Ubiquitous Moralists", a review by Ransom of Blackmur's *The Expense of Greatness*.[33] Ransom opens up the review with very high praise. "Few if any critics live who write better criticism than R. P. Blackmur; I mean subtler and deeper criticism, and sounder. He probes the poem with a keen instrument, and his judgements, so far as an adjective is ever applicable, are close enough to infallible."[34] Yet, in the body of his review Ransom suggests "an embarrassing limitation" in Blackmur; he "has no theory of poetry which is comparable in distinction with his specific judgements".[35] Blackmur has assimilated the best in critical theory, has thought long and well about it, and has applied what he knows acutely, but he has not clearly defined his critical position. He is, perhaps, too implicit in his statements of theory and too amorphous in his critical dynamism. Ransom, I think, prefers Blackmur's openness to Burke's formalism, but he wishes that Blackmur would take more of a theoretical stand so he could more easily understand him. The impossibility, however, of not being able to label Blackmur would be more of an excellence for Ransom than a deficiency.

The other reservation he has about Blackmur is that he is NOMINALLY moralistic. This, paradoxically, is one theoretical stand that Ransom can see Blackmur making. "Blackmur conceives that the poet himself is a moralist, before the critic appears, so that the faithful critic, when he does appear and set in to report a poem, must be a moralist also", says Ransom, and "coming from him it is particularly depressing".[36] Paradoxically, Ransom will later write in his essay "More Than Gesture",[37] that poetry is more than 'the language of gesture', that there are substantive as well

---

[32] *The New Criticism*, vii.
[33] *Kenyon Review*, III (Winter, 1941), 95–100.
[34] *Ibid.*, p. 95.
[35] *Ibid.*, p. 96.
[36] *Ibid.*, p. 97.
[37] "More than Gesture", *Poems and Essays*, pp. 102–8.

as formal values in poetry. Ransom thinks, in the later essay, that Blackmur's *The Language of Gesture* is too concerned with the HOW of the poem, and not enough with the 'faith', the 'passion', the substance of the poem, that is, whether the faith, the passion and the substance of the poem be moral or not. I think there is an indication, here, of some change in Ransom's thinking from 1941, when he wrote the "Ubiquitous Moralists" on Blackmur's *The Expense of Greatness*, to 1953, when he wrote "More Than Gesture" on Blackmur's *The Language of Gesture*. I do not think that it is Blackmur who decidedly changed. In *The Double Agent* (1935), in *The Expense of Greatness* (1940), in *The Language of Gesture* (1952), and in *The Lion and the Honeycomb* (1955), Blackmur exhibits a subtle and fine probing of the relation between form and content in each poem that he considers. This is "the critic's job of work" for him, and he does it well and consistently. Ransom, however, has more tolerance in 1953 with the moral substance of the poem than in 1941. In fact, in 1955 he will call the 'what' or the 'substantive' value of the poem the 'moral universal'.[38] He would never have used this phrase in the title of an essay, unless in a pejorative way, in 1941. The "Ubiquitous Moralists", for example, is a pejorative title. His apparent tolerance with moral substance may lodge in his expanded comprehension of the meaning of the word, that is, an expansion from overt didacticism to human experience. He has mellowed, it seems, both in his violent reaction to the reality of moral themes in the poem and in his expanded understanding of the word 'moral'. In this, he has drifted closer to Winters' position of seeing moral as meaning 'plausibly human'. Yet, he has never considered propaganda or explicit didacticism or abstraction as proper material for a poem. The universal must always be clothed in its metaphor and actualized by the imagination.

In speaking of actualization, I would like to return to the completion of Ransom's distinction concerning Blackmur: that he is NOMINALLY or theoretically a moralist, but ACTUALLY, "when he is going properly", not a moralist at all.[39] "I judge from the context", Ransom says, "that he requires his moral predilections

---

[38] "The Concrete Universal", *Kenyon Review*, XVII (Summer, 1955), 383–407.

[39] "Ubiquitous Moralists", *Kenyon Review*, III (Winter, 1941), 97.

to be 'actualized' or poeticized or adapted to a concrete body, but when that happens they are surely moral predilections no longer..."[40] Blackmur feels "it incumbent upon him", says Ransom, "to declare a critical position in order to have somewhere official to stand".[41] Ransom may have done his fellow critic an injustice here, for Blackmur takes a stand that it is finely wrought and more subtly demonstrated than Ransom's. As Ransom has said, Blackmur is a new critic because he is concerned with the relation of structure to experiential matter, form to content,[42] and, if you will, structure to texture. And from what I have read of R. P. Blackmur, he has never seemed to be 'desperate' about 'taking a stand'. He is vigorous, courageous and very subtle critic.

We talked of Ransom's choice of poets in the last chapter, and we are sure of whom he likes, because he actually lists his poets. He has also mentioned the critics he likes, but he has not grouped them according to the categories of major, minor-major, and minor. I would suggest, however, that any of the critics that he has written about, throughout his work, are major to him. In "Poetry 1900–1950", Hardy was his choice as the major poet of the century, and from the general tenor of his writing, I should think that Eliot and Yeats would rate over Frost and Robinson. Those are his major group of poets. As far as his rating of major critics is concerned, I have given some idea of what he thinks about William Empson, Cleanth Brooks, T. S. Eliot, I. A. Richards, Yvor Winters, Kenneth Burke and R. P. Blackmur. He also gives occasional mention to Robert Penn Warren, as in "The Inorganic Muses",[43] and to his friend and student Allen Tate, as in the opening pages of *The World's Body*, but he does not concern himself with them in the bulk of his work. The reason for this may be that on the one hand, Warren is a much younger man than Ransom—he was a student of a student of his,[44] and, it seems, did not provoke Ransom into commentary. Furthermore, Warren did not collect his critical essays on poetry into one book until 1958, so that

[40] *Ibid.*, p. 98.
[41] *Ibid.*
[42] "A Critic's Job of Work", *The Double Agent, Essays in Craft and Elucidation*, p. 270.
[43] *Kenyon Review*, V (Spring, 1943), 287–88.
[44] Warren was Tate's student at Vanderbilt.

Ransom could not peruse them and respond to them as the editor of the *Kenyon Review*. It was in that year he retired from Kenyon College. On the other hand, Allen Tate's opinions Ransom holds 'with fewest and slightest reservations',[45] so there could not be too much provocation and response in his case.

I will not be so presumptuous as to give his hierarchy of critics, because I am not sure of what he thinks. But I will review the critics that I have already grouped according to Ransom's suggested prerequisites. In the close-reading critics we have Empson, Brooks, Blackmur and Eliot, perhaps in that order. In the scholarly critics, we have preeminently T. S. Eliot; perhaps also Empson, Richards and Blackmur. In the philosophical critics, we have Blackmur in his power of assimilation and application, Burke in his subtlety of dialectic, and Winters in his logicality. Both of these last critics err, for Ransom, in their formalistic application of principle to the poem. In addition, Brooks errs in his slighting of logical unity in the poem, in preference for its attitudinal unity. Eliot errs in his dogmatism[46] and his hypertraditionalism. Richards errs — at least in his criticism of the twenties — in mistaking psychology for poetry, and Blackmur errs in his lack of critical position and in his theoretical moralism. From all this, I think Ransom would group Eliot, Richards, and Winters as the major critics of influence. These men have raised the questions that have provoked his thoughts in essay after essay. Their questions and their theories must have been important to him or he would not have wasted ink on them. Indeed, Empson, Brooks and Blackmur may be more subtle practical critics, but they have not raised the questions that have redirected a century. Of them all, I suggest that T. S. Eliot may be the critic of maximum influence for Ransom and, therefore, of maximum importance.

---

[45] *The World's Body*, p. xii.
[46] "The Historical Critic", *The New Criticism*, p. 207.

VI

CONCLUSION: A GENERAL ESTIMATE
OF RANSOM AS CRITIC

In this section, I mean to consider the major strengths and weaknesses of Ransom's criticism, in content and procedure. Paradoxically, his strength and weakness sometimes lie in the same nuance of his criticism. The first weakness that should be considered is his notion of what poetry is and the basis of his distinction between prose and poetry.

In most cases, Ransom's definitions are not complete, and contain some inept distinctions concerning the difference between prose and poetry. For example, in one text he bases his distinction between poetry and prose on the objects which the poets will to write about.[1] But does the cause of poetry lie essentially in the will? Can we will our language to be poetry instead of prose? If the answer is yes, then those with the strongest wills may write the best poetry, and those who would will to make their language distinct from prose would have it so. But the testimony of our consciousness is that poetry does not come to be through sheer volition. As there is no necessary relation between the will and poetry, so there is none between 'beloved objects' and poetry.[2] Poets often write of things which are repulsive to them, and things which are neither 'precious' nor beloved to them. Granted that Ransom means to connote by 'precious' more than it ordinarily means, when he says, "beyond price, or valued at more than market value . . . capable of exhibiting fresh aspects of a substance which is contingent and unpredictable",[3] still, the object does not seem to distinguish prose from poetry. The impress of ANY nuance of existence as made ready by the artist's intense and unique

[1] "The Tense of Poetry", *The World's Body*, pp. 236–7.
[2] "Poetry II: The Final Cause", *Kenyon Review*, IX (Autumn, 1947), 643–5.
[3] *Ibid.*, p. 643.

response to it seems to be the initial matter or object of poetry. This is the first or initial object—the poet's realization of ANY object of existence, whether it be fearful or alien, familiar or beloved. The second or final matter of poetry would be, for me, the words that give verbal shape to the artist's realization and response to existence. In short, whether language is poetry or prose depends upon the poet and not the object.

Yet, Ransom defines poetry in many ways because he speaks of it in many different contexts. If we rummage through his essays, we will discover a central insight which may be his greatest contribution to man, if not to poetic criticism. Ransom's central vision of poetry is that it is a recovery of the 'world's body'—of particular, existent objects. Poetry is "knowledge by images, reporting the fulness of particularity".[4] It is not conceptualism, but it is an existential tasting of reality. Thus, the precious object IMPLIES a power to make it precious and to realize it as existent. This power is not part of man—the discursive intellect, or merely the affections—but it is the total man, "the general sensibility",[5] that gazes and creates with an innocence that is "knowledge without desire".[6] To be in wonder about the folds of a child's ear, forever: this is the thing that Ransom is getting at. Many of his contextual definitions are insufficient for a definition of poetry, but they center about a realization that will oscillate in his reader's mind, perhaps making poets write better poetry and making men lead living lives. This emphasis on poetry as knowledge is intense in *The World's Body*, as the title obviously indicates. It may be Ransom's great and pervading contribution to letters and to man that he has urged man to love reality and not the misplaced concreteness of cold abstraction. Rather than being a nominalist, as Winters has insisted he is, Ransom may be an existentialist whose reverence for the living thing is the consuming force of his life. He has been so absorbed with the world's exquisite unpredictability that he has ordered his definition of poetry to it.

For Ransom, the poetic correlative of the unpredictability in existence is, of course, the texture of the poem. The texture is the irrelevance which overflows the determined intention of the poet's

---

[4] "A Psychologist Looks at Poetry", *The World's Body*, p. 158.

[5] "Poetry II: The Final Cause", *Kenyon Review*, IX (Autumn, 1947), 647.

[6] "Forms and Citizens", *The World's Body*, p. 45.

mind and the logical structure in the poem. As has been mentioned, this theory has opened Ransom to attacks from various critics. Kenneth Burke, for example, has this to say about Ransom's theory of irrelevancy. "Were I to suggest a slogan for his version of the poetic state, it would not be *e pluribus unum* but *ex uno plura*. . . . When he says, for instance, 'we might sum it up by saying that the poem is a loose logical structure with an irrelevant local texture,' is that really the formula for a poem? Or wouldn't it serve better as the formula for bad prose?"[7]

Burke criticizes Ransom with some justification, for Ransom's poet seems not to have sufficient spiritual control over his verbal medium. Indeed, he seems almost to back into excellence. Ransom says, at times, that it is the poet's very inability to harmonize the conception with the image and the image with the meter that results in the excellence of the poem. We have seen that in one text Ransom mentions "the last and rarest gift" of the poet—the poetic strategy of sensing the whole poem coming into being. Yet this mention does not exonerate him from statements which imply that the poet's inability to harmonize elements in the poem leads to excellence. For example, Ransom says in *The New Criticism:* "When he [the poet] cannot further reduce his meaning to language more accurately metrical, he accepts a 'last version' and allows the variations to stand. These variations, of course, present the contingency, and the unpredictability, or in one word the 'actuality,' of the world of sound."[8] Here Ransom does not seem to give sufficient reason for a well-wrought and intelligible poem. To figure forth the spontaneity of the world takes an utter and almost exhausting concentration on the part of the poet. The poem does not write itself. And the greatness of the poem does not depend on what the artist cannot do. It depends on what he can do, and what he alone, in his response to existence, does do. *Poesis* and concentration may emerge on the bright level of consciousness or live in the dark levels of the subconscious, but the poet does not back into greatness, nor does he arrive at an exquisite and powerful intelligibility by accident. The shape of the poem is not essentially 'adventitious'.[9] It is true that the artist does not know what image

[7] "Key Words For Critics", review of *The New Criticism, Kenyon Review,* IV (Winter, 1942), 131.

[8] "The Psychological Critic", *The New Criticism,* p. 318.

[9] "The Logical Critic", *The New Criticism,* p. 261.

or rhythm may burst into consciousness. This is, consciously, unpredictable, but he does attempt to fuse the image with the rhythm, and both of these with cognition in the white flame of intuitive concentration. To the degree that the image lives in the rhythm and the rhythm heightens the effect of the image, and to the degree that both image and rhythm configure the realization of the poet, to that degree do we have a good poem. The word of the poem is only the poet's, and nothing in the poem is ESSEN-TIALLY adventitious. If the elements in the poem are adventitious, the effect and cause relation between the poet and his poem is denied. I am not throwing away Ransom's theory of tensions, for it is very fertile ground for poetic speculation, but I do think that whatever art is in the poem is caused by the artistry of the poet. No word in the poem should be truly irrelevant[10] to the experience of the poem. Indeed the poem's focus may change as the poem grows, but when the poem is done, all the elements in the poem should move to enforce the effects of the poem on the reader. To the degree that any word is essentially irrelevant to the final, intelligible experience in the poem, to that degree is it an imperfect and not an excellent poem. The spontaneity and the dynamic power of "Out of the Cradle Endlessly Rocking", for example, could not be predicted before Whitman wrote the poem, but they are certainly not irrelevant to the matter of the poem. In fact Whitman's spontaneity heightens the matter of his poetry. To the degree that the spontaneity of any poem is froth, to that degree is it irrelevant and damages the poem.

This leads us to another facet of the structure-texture or prose core-tissue of irrelevancy theory of Ransom, namely: Can it be said that a prose core really exists? To me, it cannot. Ransom's prose core is a being of the mind. Texture, or the tissue of words, is really all of the poem. It is true that we talk of matter and form, content and form and prose core and tissue in the poem, but each of these pairs represents two non-autonomous elements in the poem. The elements in each pair give life to each other. The mystery of composition is, in fact, that the matter is its verbal shape and shape

---

[10] See "An Ontological Critic", *The New Criticism*, p. 280; here Ransom makes the statement that Kenneth Burke objects to with some justification, namely, "the poem is a loose logical structure with an irrelevant local texture".

has digested all the matter into itself. What I mean is that the prose argument is not a poetic reality, and that the tissue or the texture is really all that poetically exists. For example, redness nowhere really exists, but red, flowered in a rose, does exist. The tissue—the flesh of the rose—is all we know of this particular red. Ransom, it seems, has widened a needed distinction into a separation that is an aesthetical inaccuracy. The poem is one being; it is not a dualism of two beings existing in one container, or under one name. This is literary Nestorianism. The reader apprehends, hopefully, an intelligible experience or realization through the words of the poem. He then can simplify this apprehension into an abstraction which could be called (though not rightly) the content, the matter or the structure[11] of the poem. But the experience of the poem is configured in the words, and the experience is not the prose core. The poem is existentially and uniquely one being; not essentially and dualistically a tension of two beings. In saying "We do not quite know how to feel a thought. The best we can do is to conduct a thought without denying all the innocent or irrelevant feelings in the process. The dualism remains",[12] and "The composition of a poem is an operation in which the argument fights to displace the meter, and the meter to displace the argument",[13] or "In theory, the poem is a resultant of two processes which come from opposite directions",[14] Ransom seems to dissolve a needed distinction and create an unneeded separation.

I do not wish to be unfair to Ransom. He has given us critical tools in his theory of tensions which are comparable in effect to Richards' 'tenor' and 'vehicle' and probably more effective than Eliot's 'emotion' and 'feeling'. Ransom has made the poem more accessible to investigation, for though the poem is a unity, it cannot be analyzed in that pure state. In our finite condition we cannot think without distinctions which have their foundation in reality. But we must handle our distinctions deftly, so that one being with two aspects, for example, a person with a body and soul, or a poem with structure and texture, does not double itself, and become two

---

[11] Ransom uses 'structure' to mean, in many contexts, the intellectual substance of the poem; the 'what' of the poem as understood by the intellect.

[12] "The Historical Critic", *The New Criticism*, p. 184.

[13] "An Ontological Critic", *The New Criticism*, p. 295.

[14] *Ibid.*, pp. 299–300.

beings with no aspects. Perhaps these points are fine ones, but I think they should be realized when reading Ransom.

Another point in Ransom's criticism that warrants critique and full realization is his notion of the function and necessity of form. Ransom's reasoning on this point is this: that there is an essential apart-from-ness in art, that there should be a certain aesthetic distance between the artist and his creation, and between the creation and the reader. This distance, which is effected mostly by traditional forms such as meter, stanza and metaphor in poetry, separates art from utilitarian pursuits of man. Art cannot be consumed or devoured. The beloved objects of art are preserved. The recovery of the world is set before men that they may contemplate it, not in greed, but in tranquility. There is a need for aesthetic distance in society, in religion, and in poetry for Ransom, and this distance is effected by social conventions, by religious ritual and traditional poetic forms. In fact, Ransom thinks that direct and spontaneous expression in art is well nigh fatal to the artist:

> When the consensus of taste lays down the ordinance that the artist shall express himself formally, the purpose is evidently to deter him from expressing himself immediately. Or, the formal tradition intends to preserve the artist from the direct approach to his object. Behind the tradition is probably the sense that the direct approach is perilous to the artist and may become fatal. It is feared that the artist who disregards the instruction may discover at length that he has only been artless; or what is worse, that he will not make this important discovery, which will have to be made for him by the horrid way of autopsy. I suggest therefore, that an art is usually, and, probably of necessity, a kind of obliquity; that its fixed form proposes to guarantee the round-about of the artistic process, and the "aesthetic distance."[15]

This text deserves to be well thought over, but I think it is only a partial truth that cannot be applied to all poetry or all art. Ransom includes the word 'usually', but his tone is pretty well absolute: he likes his poetry by the book, with startling variations from the book. But poets such as Whitman, in the last century, and Brother Antoninus, in this century, are their own book, and the consensus of minds is that Whitman writes poetry and so does

---

[15] "Forms and Citizens", *The World's Body*, p. 32. On this point and many others see Richard H. Fogle's extended attack on the New Critics in "Romantic Bards and Metaphysical Reviewers", *English Literary History*, XII (September, 1945), 221–50.

Antoninus. In fact, they are said to have written some powerful and exquisite poetry. Whitman was influenced by Emerson and Antoninus by Jeffers, but they are themselves and no one else, and their life is their form. They adhere to no conventional forms in meter, stanza and length of line. They are, indeed, immediate and direct, such as in "Canticle to Christ in the Holy Eucharist" by Brother Antoninus. His form, here, is more compressed than Whitman's, but he swings out just the same, letting the extrinsic form be the out-pushing of the inner, living intrinsic form of the creative poetic experience.

> Sudden as the wind that breaks east out of dawn
>   this morning you struck,
> As wind that poured from the wound of dawn
>   in the valley of my beginning.
> Your look rang like the strident quail
>   like the buck that stamps in the thicket.
> Your face was the flame. Your mouth was the rinse of wine.
>   Your tongue the torrent.[16]

Antoninus is savage, overpowering, and direct in his execution, and he is an artist.[17] In short, there is truth in what Ransom says about aesthetic distance,[18] but it cannot be applied to all poets and all poetry. In the case of Brother Antoninus and Walt Whitman, I think the distance is in the sheer printed page and the intelligibility of their rhapsodic language. Language itself is the only distance that they give. Their poetry is the hot lava of experience in the intelligible mold of language.

It follows from what I have said above that I do not agree with Ransom's and Winters' theory that was given by Ransom in *The New Criticism*. Ransom says there:

---

[16] *The Crooked Lines of God* (Detroit, 1959), pp. 82–4.

[17] In *Contemporary American Poetry* (New York, 1965), pp. 85–100, Ralph Mills includes him as one of the twelve major American poets born in the twentieth century. For me, he is the most rhapsodically powerful American poet of this century, and one of the great mystic poets of all time.

[18] This can be experienced, for example, in looking upon the human body in oil paint. The body has been given distance by form and by its suffusion through the responding and creating artist's being. The itch of lust has been removed, unless intended. Whether it needs further refinement through conventional device is the question that Ransom raises. I think it does not necessarily. Ransom would say it does necessarily.

But what I mean to examine particularly in this essay on meter is the part that deals with free verse. It is the most intelligent examination of free verse that has been offered; and still better, there is in it, along with much general metrical theory, Winters' plain understanding that the local "variation," or as we might say the local musical phrase, is nothing at all unless it is a variation within a definitive scheme—this last being of course the regular metrical pattern. It is the most important principle of metrical theory.[19]

It seems to me that Ransom has failed to make a distinction between meter and rhythm. He talks only of meter and not of rhythm. Meter[20] is an accident of poetry. Without it poetry can exist. Rhythm is a property of poetry, and without it poetry cannot exist. Rhythm issues from its principle, the poet's emotive response to existence; it is the tightly or loosely controlled reverberation of emotion. To make this distinction clearer, let me give an example. Marlowe, Shakespeare, Milton, and Wordsworth all wrote, to some extent, in blank verse, but uniquely rhythmed blank verse. Their rhythms are as different as their personalities, though their meters may be very much the same. The great booming, tympanic beat of Milton is not the restrained, intense, stepping motion of Wordsworth's sonnets. The Milton of *Paradise Lost* is tidal, periodic, volcanic—his lava issues forth; Wordsworth contains his heat within the furnace of his stricter form. So there seems to be a distinction between meter and rhythm, and it is not the regular meter that is the most memorable element of sound, but the rhythm that lives in the total sonic body of the line. When one goes to the concert hall, he does not go to hear the metronome, but to hear the music. When one reads Milton he hears and responds to his music; he scans only in analysis.

Another question that is raised in response to Ransom's paragraph on the superiority of regular meter to free verse is this: Given the existence of rhythm distinguished from meter, does effective rhythm arise only from "a variation within a definite [metric] scheme"? American anthologists think not. They give Whitman more space than any other poet, and Whitman, of course, writes without a definite metrical scheme. His poetry has overpowering rhythms, as the ocean swells have rhythms, or as the *Liebestod* of *Tristan und Isolde* has rhythm, but he does not write

---

[19] "The Logical Critic", *The New Criticism*, pp. 261-2.
[20] That is, 'regular metrical pattern'.

in a definitive metrical scheme. Some of his work has an exquisite melodic deftness, for example, lines 130–143 of "Out of the Cradle Endlessly Rocking". There is a masterly control here, but it is not a control which is superimposed; it is a control which wells up from immanence, from an intuitive sense of sonic rightness. Let us listen with our inner ear.

> The Aria sinking,
> All else, continuing, the stars shining,
> The winds blowing, the notes of the birds continuous, echoing,
> With angry moans the fierce old mother incessantly moaning,
> On the sands of Paumonock's shore gray and rustling,
> The yellow half-moon enlarged, sagging down, drooping,
>   the face of the sea almost touching,
> The boy ecstatic, with his bare feet the waves,
>   with his hair the atmosphere dallying,
> The love in the heart long pent, now loose,
>   now at last tumultuously bursting,
> The aria's meaning, the ears, the soul swiftly depositing,
> The strange tears down the cheeks coursing,
> The colloquy there, the trio, each uttering,
> The undertoe, the savage old mother incessantly crying,
> The boy's soul's questions sullenly timing,
>   some drown'd secret hissing,
> To the outsetting bard.[21]

It seems to me that Whitman—a ghost who has always haunted the new critics—has fractured the universal dictum of Ransom and Winters on the necessary superiority of regular meter over free verse rhythms. Poetic effect for Whitman is not in metered regularity, but in verbalized crest and trough which are the correlative of his felt emotion.

Ransom's notion of regularity and variation from regularity is one that produces fruitful speculation and from which many poets can learn to refine the movements of their poems. Ransom introduces poets to a consideration that may imbue a discipline that will make their phrases shine. It is also stimulating to look for what Ransom points to in such poets as Hardy. This is a part of what made these poets great. But it is not what made all poets great. In short, Ransom's notion on meter is an oversimplification, and it is erroneous as a universal statement. A poet should write

[21] *The Complete Poetry of Walt Whitman*, deathbed edition (New York, 1948), I, 241–2.

as he is able: as Whitman, Jeffers, Hopkins, and Antoninus do,
or as Spenser, Herrick, Ransom, and Hardy do. The first group
writes directly in rhythm; the other writes through meter into
rhythm.

We have, thus far in this section, spoken of Ransom's deficien-
cies. This has been done because this essay, up to here, has been
principally one of exposition, subordinately, one of critique. There
was some need to raise central questions about Ransom's critical
theory in order to fully realize its consequencies and its accuracy.

Now let us pass to the general consideration of Ransom's contribution to literary criticism and the literature of poetry. I have
already indicated my attitude towards some of his contributions;
my purpose now will be to round out this subject and my attitude,
in terms of a conclusion and a summary.

The new criticism, as we understand Ransom to mean it, was not
born wholly of Ransom, for the work of Richards and Eliot pre-
dates Ransom's[22] and these men are, to some extent, new critics.
That is, a great deal of their critical energy is taken up with concentrating upon the being of the poem in itself as an object worthy
of that energy and that concentration. But these critics wear critical bifocals: Richards is much interested in the reader, and Eliot
in the dynamic literary tradition of the West. The text, and what
the text signifies, is not their total and consuming occupation.
It very nearly is for Ransom. He is an ontologist. This means
that he wants to know things (Being as particulars) as they are,
and he wants to know this poem as it is. In this respect he does not
wear critical bifocals. Though there is, indeed, a certain oscillation
in Ransom's gaze between reality and the poem, this seems to be
necessary, for the poem refers to reality, which he calls "the world's
body". So, I would say that he is not wholly, but he is centrally,
the father of the new criticism. About him turns the vortex of
the other living objectivist critics in this country. He is the one
who has hammered longest and most persistently against narcissistic criticism, and for the consideration of poetry as poetry, and
not as something else.

The new criticism was born out of Ransom's love, Ransom's
conviction, and Ransom's fortunate limitation. Love, because

[22] So does Ezra Pound, but he does not have the refined critical influence
of any of these men.

he had an INTER-EST in beings for themselves—including a poem that catches reality in the texture of its language. Conviction, because he believed that students in a literature class should encounter literature. Limitation, because he just did not have the background to do anything other than to consider the poem in itself. He was not well-read in the history of literature in 1919, and had no other choice, at that time, than to consider the text in itself. "He was not an historical scholar", says his student, Allen Tate, "and he was concerned, in talking about a literary work, with ideas and techniques. I was too ignorant to understand how. it came about that such a man should be in an English department. I doubt that he had taken more than two or three courses in English as an undergraduate at Vanderbilt; he took none later at Oxford . . . he went on to read English literature on his own."[23]

Ransom moved, from this beginning, against what I have called narcissistic criticism. Northrop Frye has also used this term,[24] though his use of 'narcissistic' may not coincide exactly with mine. I use the term in the sense that the neo-Freudian Erich Fromm uses it in *The Art of Loving*.[25] Here Fromm explains that only by humility and reason can one emerge from various illusionary levels of supposed omniscience and omnipotence. Reason and humility will lead man to the daylight of objectivity—to things, not as we would have them or as we fear them or as we have thought them to be, but as they are: to the knowledge of being, including the poem, as it is; to the knowledge of being so that we may love it and live for it. I take this neo-Freudian view of Ransom's theories because I think it gives a penetrating insight into the truth that Ransom has sought and has tried to give to the literary world. He does not seek to superimpose his own morals, his own preoccupations or fears on the world or on the poem, which recovers the world through words. Psychologism, moralism, and even historicism are self-seeking appetites, for Ransom, when they saturate a critic's mind. Richards, Winters, and Eliot—the critics that Ransom is most preoccupied with—have not come fully into the light of Being. They are not fully reasonable critics for Ransom

[23] "For John Crowe Ransom at Seventy-five", *Shenandoah*, XIV (Spring, 1963), 5–8.
[24] "Criticism, Visible and Invisible", *College English*, XXVI (October, 1964), 9.
[25] *The Art of Loving* (New York, 1956), p. 118.

because they are not fully ontological critics; they have forsaken the world for a bias. They are in some degree inhibited by the security they feel in their psychologistic, moralistic, and Christian-historical assumptions. What Ransom wants is an emergence from bias and the awakening of an alert sensibility that will respond to the world and the poem as they are: the world as the total fullness of particular being and the poem as an aesthetical being with an ontological reference. The texture of the poem, for Ransom, is a testimony of the poet's faithfulness to reality and to himself, as part of reality. Ransom is almost willing to let the poem go its own unpredictable way, as the world is free to go. In his dialectical fashion, he refuses to assume any degree of critical omniscience or omnipotence. He does not seek to superimpose Platonic forms upon a world that does not fit them, nor will he seek to manipulate things in the scientific exercise of power. He and the poet are subject to the world, and the world is subject to them in their wonder and in their worded creation.

Finally, in his critical procedure he is always incomplete because he is always dialectical—he has never come, he believes, and will never come to the whole truth about anything. Thus, he is irritating in his incompleteness, but there is a reason for it. He will not attempt an exhaustive definition of poetry, perhaps, because there is none. Knowledge has an open end for Ransom.

As is evidenced in *The New Criticism*, Ransom has read Eliot long and hard, and his style resembles Eliot's. For example, neither Ransom nor Eliot is particularly logical in his critical progression. They lack the order which the mind urges when reading them. They do not define, divide, and discuss very systematically. Both critics intimate a part of a definition, make somewhat arbitrary divisions, and then discuss what they are interested in, with a casual unpredictability.[26] I hope I am not discourteous in saying that they remind me of two venerable beachcombers who search through the sands of texts, sifting them, comparing one item with another,

---

[26] In order to give a proper reference here I would have to refer to the entire bulk of these critics' writings, for this is a question of their general procedure; however, as an example of this procedure, I refer to the reader to Eliot's essay "The Function of Criticism", *Selected Essays* (New York, 1950), pp. 12–22 and Ransom's essay "Shakespeare at Sonnets", *The World's Body*, pp. 270–303, both of which contain oversimplified attacks on Romantic poetry.

and unexpectedly come up with a gem of an insight, an insight with a memorable formulation: 'structure' and 'texture', 'dissociation of sensibility', 'tissue of irrelevancy', 'objective correlative', and so on. Neither critic has the philosophic vision of a Lovejoy or a Frye, and neither has the finely honed critical scalpel of a Black-mur, but their insights are begotten of a deep and far-ranging sensi-bility. They have been up and down the beach many times, and when they have discovered something in the sand, one can be sure that it is the result of much labor, much knowledge, and much sensibility. They are not the type to make razor-sharp distinction after distinction. They have neither the desire nor the specific power to be a Maritain. Eliot's strength is in the incomparable breadth of his literary and non-literary knowledge, combined with an intimate knowledge of the poem from the creative inside of it. Ransom's strength is in his combination of a scholarship not as broad as Eliot's, with a poetic sensibility comparable to Eliot's, in addition to an existential philosopher's interest in existing things.

Ransom has given the critical world a redirection—not by him-self, but centrally by the persistence of his critical writing in the journal which he began and astutely edited, *The Kenyon Review*. He has made the pragmatists clear their vision again and again, and made them focus upon the poem, whose reason for existence, he thinks, is to catch up the world beautifully in the texture of its worded being.

A SELECTED BIBLIOGRAPHY

Abrams, M. H., "Unconscious Expectations in the Reading of Poetry", *English Literary History*, IX (December, 1942) 235–44.

—, *The Mirror and the Lamp: Romantic Theory and the Critical Tradition* (New York, Oxford University Press, 1953).

Ames, Van Meter, "Expression and Aesthetic Expression", *Journal of Aesthetics and Art Criticism*, VI (December, 1947), 172–9.

Antoninus, Brother, *The Crooked Lines of God* (Detroit, University of Detroit Press, 1959).

Aristotle, *The Poetics. Basic Works of Aristotle*, ed. Richard McKeon (New York: Random House Inc., 1941).

Barrett, William, "The Temptation of St. Yvor", *Kenyon Review*, IX (Autumn, 1947), 532–48.

Bate, Walter Jackson, ed., *Criticism: The Major Texts* (New York and Burlingame, Harcourt Brace and World Inc., 1952).

Battestin, Martin, C., "John Ransom and Lycidas: A Reappraisal", *College English*, XVII (December, 1956), 223–228.

Bergson, Henri, *The Creative Mind* (New York, The Philosophical Library, 1946).

Blackmur, R. P., *The Double Agent, Essays in Craft and Elucidation* (New York, Arrow Editions, 1935).

—, "In Our Ends Are Our Beginnings", *Virginia Quarterly Review*, XIV (Summer, 1938), 445–50.

—, *The Expense of Greatness* (New York, Arrow Editions, 1940).

—, *Language as Gesture, Essays in Poetry* (New York, Harcourt, Brace and Co., 1952).

Blum, Morgan, "The Fugitive Particular", *Wiseman Review*, XIV (1950), 85–102.

Bosanquet, Bernard, *A History of Aesthetics from the Greeks to the 20th Century* (New York, MacMillan Co., 1932).

Bradbury, John, *The Fugitives, A Critical Account* (Chapel Hill, University of North Carolina Press, 1958).

Brooks, Cleanth, *Modern Poetry and the Tradition* (Chapel Hill, University of North Carolina Press, 1939).

—, *The Well Wrought Urn, Studies in the Structure of Poetry* (New York, Harcourt, Brace and Co., Harvest Books, 1947).

—, "Homage to John Crowe Ransom", *Shenandoah*, XIV (Spring 1963), 9.

Buchanan, Scott, "The Search for the Trinity", *Virginia Quarterly Review*, VII (July, 1931), 457–61.

Burke, Kenneth, *Counterstatement* (New York, Harcourt, Brace and Co., 1931).

—, "On Poetry and Poets", *Poetry*, LV (October, 1939), 50–54.

—, "Key Words for Critics", a review of *The New Criticism*, *Kenyon Review*, IV (Winter, 1942), 126–32.

—, *A Grammar of Motives* (New York, Prentice-Hall Inc., 1945).

—, *The Philosophy of Literary Form, Studies in Symbolic Action* (Baton Rouge, Louisiana State University Press, 1942).

Coleridge, S. T., *Biographia Literaria*, ed. J. Shawcross, 2 vols. (Oxford, Clarendon Press, 1907).

Cowan, Louise, *The Fugitive Group: A Literary History* (Baton Rouge, Louisiana State University Press, 1959).

Cowie, Alexander, "Esthetic Experience", *Saturday Review of Literature*, XXIV (July, 1941), 13.

Crane, Ronald S., *Critics and Criticism* (Chicago, University of Chicago Press, 1952).

Croce, Benedetto, "Aesthetics", *Encyclopedia Britannica*, 14th ed., rev., I, 265–66 (Chicago, London and Toronto, Encyclopedia Britannica Inc., 1952).

Deutsch, Babette, *This Modern Poetry* (New York, W. W. Norton, 1935).

Dupee, F. W., Review of *Selected Poems* by John Crowe Ransom, *The Nation*, CLXI (August 11, 1945), 138–9.

Eliot, T. S., *Selected Essays* (New York, Harcourt, Brace and Co., 1950).

Empson, William, *Seven Types of Ambiguity*, 2nd ed. rev. and reset (New York, New Directions, 1947).

Fogle, Richard H., "Romantic Bards and Metaphysical Reviewers", *English Literary History*, XII (September, 1945), 221–50.

Ford, Newell F., "Empson's and Ransom's Mutations of Texts", *Philological Quaterly*, XXXIX (October, 1950), 81–84.

Fromm, Erich, *The Art of Loving* (New York, World Perspectives, 1956).

Frye, Northrop, "Criticism, Visible and Invisible", *College English*, XXVI (October, 1964), 3–12.

Gamble, Isabel, "Ceremonies in Bravery", *Hopkins Review*, VI (Spring–Summer), 105–115.

Graves, Robert, Review of *Chills and Fever* by John Crowe Ransom, *Saturday Review of Literature*, I (December 27, 1924), 412.

Handy, William J., "The Ontological Theory of the Ransom Critics", *University of Tennessee Studies in English*, XXXV (1956), 32–50.

Hofstader, A. and R. Kuhns, eds., *Philosophies of Art and Beauty* (New York, Random House Inc., 1964).

Hough, Graham, "Marvell of the Deep South", *Listener*, LXIV (1960), 183–5.

—, "John Crowe Ransom: The Poet and Critic", *Southern Review*, I (Winter, 1965), 1–21.

Hulme, T. E., "Romanticism and Classicism", *Speculations, Essays on Humanism and the Philosophy of Art*, ed. Herbert Read, 2nd ed. (New York, Harcourt, Brace and Co. Inc., 1936).

126   A SELECTED BIBLIOGRAPHY

Hyman, Stanley Edgar, *The Armed Vision, A Study in the Methods of Literary Criticism* (New York, Alfred A. Knopf, 1948).

James, D. G., *Skepticism and Poetry* (London, Allen and Unwin Ltd., 1937).

Jones, Howard Mumford, *The Theory of American Literature*, Rev. ed. (Ithaca, Cornell University Press, 1965).

Kant, Immanuel, *Gesamelte Schriften*, 23 bds. (Berlin, George Reimer, 1910).

Kazin, Alfred, "Criticism at the Poles", *New Republic*, CVII (October 19, 1942), 492–99.

—, *On Native Grounds, An Interpretation of Modern American Prose Literature* (New York, Reynal and Hitchcock, 1942).

Keats, John, *Keats' Complete Poetical Works and Letters*, ed. H. E. Scudder (Cambridge, Houghton Mifflin Co., 1899).

Knickerbocker, W. S., "Wam for Maw: Dogma Versus Discursiveness in Criticism". *Sewanee Review*, XLIX (October, 1941), 520–36.

Krieger, Murray, *The New Apologists for Poetry* (Minneapolis, University of Minnesota Press, 1956).

Lemon, L. T., *The Partial Critics* (New York, Oxford University Press, 1965).

Lessing, Götthold Ephraim, *Laocoön*, trans. and ed. E. A. McCormick (Indianapolis, Bobbs-Merrill Co. Inc., 1962).

Lowell, Robert, "John Ransom's Conversation", *Sewanee Review*, LVI (July-September, 1948), 374–77.

Mac Leish, Archibald, *Collected Poems, 1917–52* (New York, Houghton Mifflin and Co., 1952).

Maritain, Jacques, *Creative Intuition in Art and Poetry* (New York, Pantheon Books Inc., 1953).

Mathiessen, F. O., "American Poetry 1920–40", *Sewanee Review*, LV (Winter, 1947), 24–55.

Mill, John Stuart, *Dissertations and Discussions*, 2 vols. (London, John W. Parker and Son, 1859–67).

Mills, Gordon Harrison, *Myth and Ontology in the Thought of John Crowe Ransom* (Dissertation, State University of Iowa, 1942).

Mills, Ralph, *Contemporary American Poetry* (New York, Random House Inc., 1965).

Mizener, Arthur, "Recent Criticism", *Southern Review*, V (Autumn, 1939), 376–400.

—, Review of *Selected Poems* by John Crowe Ransom, *Quarterly Review of Literature*, II (1945), 366–7.

Muir, Edwin, "English Poets and Others", *Saturday Review of Literature*, I (June 6, 1925), 807.

Norton, Daniel S., Review of *Selected Poems* by John Crowe Ransom, *Virginia Quaterly Review*, XXII (Summer, 1946), 438–47.

Plato, *Ion. Dialogues of Plato*, 3rd ed., ed. and trans. Benjamin Jowett, 2 vols. (New York, Random House Inc., 1937).

Poe, Edgar Allan, *The Complete Works of Edgar Allan Poe*, ed. J. A. Harrison, Virginia ed. 17 vols. (New York, AMS Press, 1965).

Pottle, F. A., "Theory of Poetry", *Yale Review*, XXVIII (Autumn, 1938), 183–5.

Raine, Kathleen, "The Poetic Symbol", *Southern Review*, I (Winter, 1965), 243–58.

Raiziss, Sona, *The Metaphysical Passion, Seven Modern American Poets and the Seventeenth Century Tradition* (Philadelphia, University of Pennsylvania Press, 1952).

Ransom, John Crowe, Editorial, *The Fugitive*, I (October, 1922), 66–68.

—, "The Future of Poetry", *The Fugitive*, III (February, 1924), 2–4.

—, "Flux and Blur in Contemporary Art", *Sewanee Review*, XXXVII (July, 1929), 353–66.

—, "Classical and Romantic", *Saturday Review of Literature*, VI (September, 1929), 125–7.

—, "Reconstructed but Unregenerate", *I'll Take My Stand: The South and the Agrarian Tradition by Twelve Southerners* (New York, Harper & Brothers, 1930), pp. 1–27.

—, Review of *The Realm of Matter* by George Santayana, *New Republic*, LXIV (October 22, 1930), 262–3.

—, *God Without Thunder: An Unorthodox Defense of Orthodoxy* (New York and London, Charles Scribner's Sons, 1930).

—, "A Poem Nearly Anonymous", *American Review*, I (May, 1933), 179–203.

—, "Forms and Citizens", *American Review*, I (September, 1933), 444–67.

—, Introduction. *Daemon in the Rock* by Edwin R. Frost (New York, G. P. Putnam's Sons, 1934).

—, "The Aesthetic of Regionalism", *American Review*, II (January, 1934), 290–310.

—, Review of *The Use of Poetry* by T. S. Eliot, *Saturday Review of Literature*, X (March 24, 1934), 574.

—, "Poetry: A Note on Ontology", *American Review*, III (May, 1934), 172–200.

—, "Poets Without Laurels", *Yale Review*, XXIV (Autumn, 1934), 503–18.

—, "Modern with the Southern Accent", *Virginia Quarterly Review*, II (April, 1935), 184–200.

—, "The Cathartic Principle", *American Review*, V (Summer, 1935), 287–300.

—, "Poetic Strategy", review of *Golden Fleece* by W. R. Benet, *Saturday Review of Literature*, XII (July 27, 1935), 6.

—, "The Mimetic Principle", *American Review*, V (October, 1935), 536–51.

—, "The Tense of Poetry", *Southern Review*, I (Autumn, 1935), 221–38.

—, "Characters and Character", *American Review*, VI (January, 1936), 271–88.

—, "Contemporaneous Not Contemporary", *Southern Review*, II (Autumn, 1936), 339–418.

—, "A Cathedralist Looks at Murder". *Southern Review*, I (Winter, 1936), 609–23.

—, "Sentimental Exercise", *Yale Review*, XXVI (December, 1936), 353–68.

—, "The Making of a Modern: The Poetry of George Marion O'Donnell", *The Southern Review*, I (Spring, 1936), 864–74.

—, "The Poet as Woman", *Southern Review*, II (Spring, 1937), 783–88.

—, "Art and Mr. Santayana", *Virginia Quarterly Review*, XIII (Summer, 1937), 420–36.

—, "Criticism Inc.", *Virginia Quarterly Review* (Autumn, 1937), 586–602.

—, "Mr. Empson's Muddles", *Southern Review*, VI (Autumn, 1938), 322–39.

—, *The World's Body* (New York and London, Charles Scribner's Sons, 1938).

—, "Arts and the Philosophers", *Kenyon Review*, I (Spring, 1939), 194-99.

—, "Yeats and His Symbols", *Kenyon Review*, I (Summer, 1939), 309–22.

—, "The Teaching of Poetry", *Kenyon Review*, I (Winter, 1939), 81–83.

—, "Apologia for Modernism", a review of *Modern Poetry and the Tradition* by Cleanth Brooks, *Kenyon Review*, II (Spring, 1940), 247–51.

—, "Honey and Gall", *Southern Review*, VI (Summer, 1940), 2–19.

—, "The Pragmatics of Art", *Kenyon Review*, II (Winter, 1940), 76–87.

—, "Happy Farmers", *Contemporary Southern Prose*, ed. Richard C. Beatty and W. P. Fidler (Boston, D. C. Heath and Co., 1940), pp. 150–66.

—, "Eliot and the Metaphysicals", *Accent*, I (Spring, 1941), 148–56.

—, "The Younger Poets", *Kenyon Review*, III (Autumn, 1941), 491–94.

—, "The Aesthetic of Music", *Kenyon Review*, III (Autumn, 1941), 494–97.

—, "The Irish, the Gaelic, the Byzantine", *Southern Review*, VII (Winter, 1941), 517–46.

—, "Ubiquitous Moralists", *Kenyon Review*, III (Winter, 1941), 95–100.

—, "Criticism as Pure Speculation", *The Intent of the Critic*, ed. Donald Stauffer (Princeton, Princeton University Press, 1941), pp. 91–124.

—, "Yvor Winters: The Logical Critic", *Southern Review*, VI (Winter, 1941), 558–83.

—, *The New Criticism* (Norfolk, Connecticut, New Directions, 1941).

—, "An Address to Kenneth Burke", *Kenyon Review*, IV (Spring, 1942), 218–37.

—, "The Inorganic Muses", *Kenyon Review*, V (Spring, 1943,) 278–300.

—, "Positive and Near-Positive Aesthetics", *Kenyon Review*, V (Summer, 1943), 443–47.

—, "The Bases of Criticism", *Sewanee Review*, LII (Autumn, 1944), 556–71.

—, "Art Needs a Little Separating", *Kenyon Review*, VI (Winter, 1944), 114–22.

—, *Review of A Grammar of Motives* by Kenneth Burke, *New Republic*, CXIV (February 18, 1946), 257–8.

—, "On Shakespeare's Language", *Sewanee Review*, LV (Summer, 1947), 181–98.

—, "Poetry: The Formal Analysis", *Kenyon Review*, IX (Summer, 1947), 436–56.

—, "Poetry: II, The Final Cause", *Kenyon Review*, IX (Autumn, 1947), 640–58.

—, "Art Worries the Naturalists", *Kenyon Review*, VII (Summer, 1948), 382–402.

—, "Understanding of Fiction", *Kenyon Review*, XII (Spring, 1950), 189–215.

—, "The Poetry of 1900–1950", *Kenyon Review*, XIII (Summer, 1951), 445–454.

—, "Why Critics Don't Go Mad", *Kenyon Review*, XIV (Spring, 1952), 331–39.

—, "Humanism at Chicago", *Kenyon Review*, XIV (Autumn, 1952), 647–659.

—, "The Concrete Universal: Observations on the Understanding of Poetry I", *Kenyon Review*, XVI (Autumn, 1954), 554–564.

—, "The Concrete Universal: Observations on the Understanding of Poetry II", *Kenyon Review* (Summer, 1955), 383–407.

—, *Poems and Essays* (New York, Vintage Books Inc., 1955).

—, "New Poems and Old Muses", *American Poetry at Mid-Century* (Washington, The Library of Congress, 1958), pp. 1–14.

—, "The Idea of a Literary Anthropologist and What He Might Say of the 'Paradise Lost' of John Milton", *Kenyon Review*, XXI (Spring, 1960), 169–193.

—, "Thomas Hardy's Poems", *Kenyon Review*, XXV (Spring, 1960), 169–193.

Richards, I. A., *Principles of Literary Criticism* (London, K. Paul, Trench, Trubner and Co., Ltd., 1924).

—, *Practical Criticism, A Study in Literary Judgement* (London, K. Paul, Routledge Ltd., 1929).

Robeson, Helen, *John Crowe Ransom, Dualist* (M. A. Thesis, Vanderbilt University, 1944).

Roellinger, Francis X., Jr., "Two Theories of Poetry as Knowledge", *Southern Review*, VII (Spring, 1942), 690–705.

Rubin, Louis D., Jr., "John Ransom's Cruel Battle", *Shenandoah*, IX (1958), 23–5.

Schopenhauer, Arthur, *The World as Will and Idea*, trans. R. B. Haldane and J. Kemp, 3 vols. (London, K. Paul, Trench, Trubner and Co., Ltd., 1891).

Schwartz, Delmore, "The Poetry of Allen Tate", *Southern Review*, V (Winter, 1940), 419–38.

—, "Instructed of Much Mortality: A Note on the Poetry of John Crowe Ransom", *Sewanee Review*, LIV (Summer, 1946), 438–48.

Schorer, Mark *et al*, *Criticism: The Foundations of Modern Literary Judgement* (New York, Harcourt, Brace and Co., 1948).

Smith, Bernard, *Forces in American Criticism* (New York, Harcourt, Brace and Co., 1939).

Spencer, Theodore, "A Critique of Poetry", *New Republic*, XCVI (August 10, 1938), 27–8.

Spiller, Robert E. *et al.*, *Literary History of the U.S.* (New York, The Macmillan Co., 1960).

Stallman, Robert Wooster, "John Crowe Ransom: A Checklist", *Sewanee Review*, LVI (July–September, 1948), 442–476.

—, *Critiques and Essays in Criticism, 1920–1948* (New York, Ronald Press Co., 1949).

Stevens, Wallace, "John Crowe Ransom: Tennesseean", *Sewanee Review*, LVI (July–September, 1948), 367–9.

Stewart, J. L., *John Crowe Ransom* (Minneapolis, University of Minnesota Press, 1962).

Tate, Allen, "The Eighteenth Century South", *Nation*, CXXIV (March 30, 1927), 346.

—, Editorial Note, *Sewanee Review*, LVI (July–September, 1948), 366.

—, *Collected Essays* (Denver, Allan Swallow, 1959).

—, "For John Crowe Ransom at Seventy-five", *Shenandoah*, XIV (Spring, 1963), 5–8.

Tennyson, Alfred, *The Poetical Works of Alfred Tennyson* (Chicago, National Library Association, 1895).

Van O'Connor, William, "The World as Body", *Sewanee Review* (July–September, 1948), 435–441.

Warren, Robert Penn, "Note on Three Southern Poets", *Poetry*, XL (May, 1932), 103–13.

—, "Pure and Impure Poetry", *Kenyon Review*, V (Spring, 1943), 228–34.

—, "John Crowe Ransom: Some Random Remarks", *Shenandoah*, XIV (Spring, 1963), 19–21.

Whitman, Walt, *Complete Poetry and Selected Prose*, ed. James E. Miller, Jr. (Boston, Houghton Mifflin Co., 1959).

—, *The Complete Poems of Walt Whitman*, deathbed ed., 2 vols. (New York, Pellegrini and Cudahy, 1948).

Wilson, Edmund, Review of *Two Gentlemen in Bonds. New Republic*, XLIX (February 2, 1927), 310.

Wimsatt, W. K., "The Structure of the Concrete Universal", *PMLA*, LXII (March, 1947), 262–80.

—, *The Verbal Icon, Studies in the Meaning of Poetry.* (Lexington, University of Kentucky Press, 1954).

— and Cleanth Brooks, *Literary Criticism, A Short History* (New York, Alfred A. Knopf, 1962).

Winters, Yvor, *In Defense of Reason* (Denver, Allan Swallow, 1947).

Wordsworth, William, *Preface to the Second Addition of the Lyrical Ballads*, eds. R. L. Brett and A. R. Jones (New York, Barnes and Noble, 1963).

Wright, William K., *A History of Modern Philosophy* (New York, The Macmillan Co., 1941).

Young, Edward, *Conjectures on Original Composition*, ed. Edith J. Morley (New York, Longmans, Green and Co., 1918).

Zabel, Morton D., *Literary Opinion in America*, 2 vols. (New York and Evanston, Harper and Row, Torch Books, 1962).

INDEX